THE LAST
THIRTY DAYS

THE LAST
THIRTY DAYS

The War Diary of the German Armed Forces High Command from April to May 1945

The Battle for Berlin

Reflections on the Events of 1945

Joachim Schultz-Naumann

Translated by D. G. Smith

MADISON BOOKS
Lanham • New York • London

English translation

Copyright © 1991 by Madison Books

Published by Madison Books
4720 Boston Way
Lanham, Maryland 20706

3 Henrietta Street
London WC2E 8LU England

Distributed by National Book Network

The paper used in this publication meets the minimum
requirements of American National Standard for
Information Sciences—Permanence of Paper for
Printed Library Materials, ANSI Z39.48–1984. ∞™
Manufactured in the United States of America.

Original German text, Die Letzten Dreissig Tage
published by Universitas Verlag, Munich,
Federal Republic of Germany

Library of Congress Cataloging-in-Publication Data

Schultz-Naumann, Joachim.
[Letzten dreissig Tage. English]
The last thirty days : the war diary of the German Armed
Forces High Command from April to May 1945 : the battle
for Berlin : reflections on the events of 1945 / Joachim
Schultz-Naumann ; translated by D.G. Smith.
p. cm.
Includes index.
1. Berlin, Battle of, 1945—Sources.
I. Title. II. Title: Last 30 days.
D757.9.B4S3813   1989
940.54'21—dc20   89-9156 CIP

ISBN 0–8191–7729–6 (alk. paper)

British Cataloging in Publication Information Available

To my fellow soldiers,
known and unknown,
wherever their graves may be
and under whatever flag.

The War Diary contained in this book first appeared in 1951 in the series "Dokumente zur Zeitgeschichte" (Documents in Contemporary History), Steingrüben-Verlag, Stuttgart, published by Jürgen Thorwald under the title "Joachim Schultz, Die letzten 30 Tage. Aus dem Kriegstagebuch des OKW."

Photo Credits

Bibliothek für Zeitgeschichte, Stuttgart
Photos 5, 6, 19, 21, 23, 25, 26, 27, 28

Bildarchiv Preussischer Kulturbesitz, Berlin, Photo 11

Bilderdienst Süddeutscher Verlag, Munich
Photos 12, 15, 16, 18, 24, 34

Hans Dollinger, Munich, Photos 1, 2, 9, 13

Flensburger Tageblatt, Photo 14

Imperial War Museum, London, Photos 3, 4

Marineschule Mürwik, Photo 7

Meyer-Detring, General a.D., Photo 8

Joachim Schultz-Naumann, Photos 10, 22, 30, 31, 32, 33

Ullstein Bilderdienst, Berlin, Photos 17, 20, 35

Maps: Joachim Schultz-Naumann

Contents

A section of photos follows page 94.

Preface

My book is addressed to American and British readers almost fifty years after World War II. It is not the purpose of this work to present a comprehensive history of the final phase of the Second World War. However, the contemporary records and the dramatic narrative of somber events presented here retain their relevance as testimony of a distant episode in an era of history with revolutionary and momentous consequences.

The War Diary of the Last Thirty Days

I was thirty-one years old when I commenced writing the War Diary of the Wehrmacht High Command. This diary was first published in 1951 and again in 1980 together with the report documenting "The Battle for Berlin" and "Reflections on the Events of 1945." The keeping of the War Diary during World War II for the top-level military staff was the specific task of the Major of the Reserve, Percy Schramm, professor of history. In April 1945, he was sent to the Southern Defense Zone of Germany, whilst the decisive political and military events were taking place in northern Germany. At that time I was appointed to keep the official War Diary of the High Command of the German Armed Forces owing to my having studied history before the war. After having fought in Poland, France, Russia, Italy and Germany, being severely wounded several times and having lost one of my legs, I came as Major of the General Staff to the Armed Forces Operations Staff, which moved from the headquarters in Zossen, south of Berlin, to Flensburg Mürwik in the north close to the German–Danish border. After arriving at the new headquarters located in the Naval School at Mürwik, I began to record the daily events of the war: operations of the enemy, operations of German troops, and joint operations involving all branches of the armed forces. I reproduced a complete picture of everything that happened by attending the daily situation conferences where I had access to the basic information. By concentrating on essentials, it was possible not only to portray the sequence of events, but also to clarify the justification behind command decisions and their effects. As only experts are familiar with the concise military style of writing, I decided to produce a revised edition of my diary to make the text more readable. Judgements and evaluations have been incorporated in this edition reflecting future developments and taking these aspects into account or assuming knowledge of them. An appendix contains the original war diary entries for April 29 and May 3, 1945 (including the Wehrmacht reports for both dates) to provide examples of the original documents and to permit comparisons to be made.

The Battle for Berlin

My account reflects both chronologically and factually the experiences of those most personally involved. I remember vividly when General Jodl, Chief of the Armed Forces Operations Staff, was able to obtain Hitler's permission to reverse the entire front facing the Americans and the British, to throw these forces into the Battle for Berlin and to control the battle directly from the Wehrmacht High Command. My report of the threat to Berlin, its encirclement and fall is comparable with the War Diary of the last thirty days and fits into the pattern of the large-scale events.

Reflections on the Events of 1945

In these reflections, I recreate the final phase of the war in the Wehrmacht Operations Staff and describe my personal experiences at that time.

In order to make the events understandable to the reader, I have limited my memories to my own personal feelings. Today's readers are hardly in a position to assess the situation and personal experience of total dictatorship and totalitarianism during and especially at the end of the war. They have grown up in a free world where there are no fatal consequences to be feared from expressing different opinions to those imposed by the state. Therefore the modern reader can scarcely understand that the Germans continued to fight until the bitter end.

As experienced officers posted at the front, we failed to understand Hitler's often senseless orders to keep holding out. We did not yield to the shabby propaganda to which many others were already succumbing. Most of us had a premonition that Hitler was a semi-cultured amateur who had abused us as soldiers. The name "Hitler" had no relevance as far as we were concerned—we were fighting for the continued existence of our native country. That was the most decisive point for us.

The desperate fight of the Germans against the Red Army in 1945 proved to be imperative to the existence of Europe. We simply refused to believe that the Western Allies would make as many concessions to the Soviets as they did in Yalta in February 1945. When the Red Army invaded Germany, an outburst of rage on the part of Soviet soldiers took place which defied all laws of humanity. The fear of the Germans was tremendous; everybody was trying to save his own life. The Red Army indiscriminatingly raped women, plundered and murdered. Now that the Iron Curtain has been torn down, Germans and Russians are no longer separated from one another by fear. But in April–May 1945 the Germans were determined to continue the fight to the finish against the Red Army. This is convincingly explained in the documentation presented.

In May 1945 a political end to the war was therefore impossible under the circumstances of that time. Most of the Germans were not able to free themselves from the irrational will to hold out, intensified by the demand of unconditional surrender. Therefore the question as to whether the high losses and destruction could have been avoided is superfluous. In retrospect, one may reconsider many events from a different point of view. But as the chronicler who saw how the machinery of war became coordinated at the end, I cannot imagine a more favorable conclusion of this somber chapter of German history.

The events of that time show the skepticism of the Allies toward the Red Army. On the first of May 1945 for example, the commander of a British-Canadian advance force, which had conquered the city of Wismar on the Baltic Sea, ordered the German troops to maintain the frontline east of the city against the Russians until British reinforcements could arrive. Evidently the British-Canadian troops were glad that the Germans were able to hold the front. Realistically minded British and American officers had foreseen the tensions that existed and would grow stronger between East and West. I personally became acquainted with this when conversing with them in Flensburg-Mürwik.

Looking back to the day of the unconditional surrender, when the German High Command gave orders to suspend active operations at 2301 hours Central European Time on 8 May 1945, I call to mind the words of John Colville, Chief of the Personal Office of Churchill in World War II. In his book *Fringes of Power: Downing Street Diaries 1939–1955,* Colville renders his impartial evaluation of the German soldier as being the best in the world.

Today Americans, British and Germans emerge as victors of the Cold War which commenced after 1945. A unified Germany will become a free and safe place to live if the Atlantic Alliance remains steadfast and Europe becomes united. If the Soviet Empire really collapses, many suppressed countries will again become free nations. This should put an end to conflicts in Europe.

These are the reflections of an officer, then a young man of thirty-one, now seventy-seven years old, who as a patriot has fought and suffered for his Fatherland.

Joachim Schultz-Naumann

PART ONE

The Last Thirty Days in the Wehrmacht High Command April–May 1945

April 20, 1945

On April 20, 1945 the last act of the dramatic collapse of the German armed forces began in the military command headquarters.

The leading elements of the Russian tank formations have penetrated to the area of Baruth, 18 kilometers south of Zossen, for many years the seat of the Wehrmacht High Command (OKW), the Wehrmacht Operations Staff, and the Army General Staff.

On the morning of April 20, 1945, the Deputy Chief of the Wehrmacht Operations Staff, Major General Winter, gives an address on the occasion of Hitler's birthday and mentions the possibility that the war could have a negative outcome. This is the first time that such an opinion is aired before a large, internal circle.

On April 20, the Wehrmacht Operations Staff represents the situation on the fronts as follows:

The Kurland front and the remaining East Prussian front on the Hela Peninsula and in the Vistula basin are being held against heavy Russian attacks. The coastal fortress of Pillau is the target of superior enemy attacks. The Oder front is now only being held against Soviet assaults on both sides of Frankfurt/Oder and between Schwedt and Stettin where the Army Group Vistula, commanded by General Heinrici, succeeded in turning back the attacks of the First Belorussian Front of Marshal Zhukov and the Second Belorussian Front of Marshal Rokossovsky. Marshal Zhukov's forces have penetrated deep into the German defenses with their leading elements in the outskirts, east of Berlin.

In bitter defensive actions along the Fürstenwalde-Straussberg-Bernau line, we are trying to halt the enemy advance. Despite the fact that our combat groups—clinging to natural obstacles and townships in the area between Görlitz and Frankfurt/Oder—are stubbornly resisting the enemy, Marshal Konev and his First Ukrainian Front have penetrated as far as the Görlitz-Bautzen area and have by-passed Spremberg in the direction of Kamenz. Between Spremberg and Cottbus he has achieved a decisive breakthrough to a point south of the capital. Here leading enemy tank units have reached the area of Jüterbog and Wünsdorf. For the Ninth German Army fighting in the area south of Berlin, this day is the beginning of an agonizing fourteen-day period of an encirclement and breakout battle.

General Rendulic's Army Group South has beaten off the assault of the Third Ukrainian Front of Marshal Tolbukhin in the area of St. Pölten. Army Group Center (Field Marshal Schörner) has also been able to hold the assaults of the Second Ukrainian Front (Marshal Malinovsky) and the Fourth Ukrainian Front (General Eremenko) in the Bohemia–Moravia area in the general line of Mistelbach (north of Vienna)–Brünn–Mährisch–Ostrau.

Fortress Breslau, which has been encircled since February 17, continues to defeat strong enemy attacks. On the Atlantic, the isolated coastal fortresses of Gironde North and Gironde South have fallen after running out of ammunition. The fortresses of St. Nazaire and Lorient are able to hold out until the capitulation.

In the northwest of the Reich, now commanded by (Commander in Chief Northwest, Field Marshal Busch), the 21st British Army Group (Commander in Chief Field Marshal Montgomery), with the First Canadian Army, are attacking on the lower Ems in the area of Papenburg–Friesoythe. After breaking German resistance, parts of the First Canadian Army are in north and east Holland on the Grebbe Line, which is being held by the troops of General Blaskowitz (the defender of Fortress Holland).

The Second British Army (also part of the 21st British Army Group) is attacking Delmenhorst and Bremen with its left wing and meeting stiff German resistance, while its right wing—advancing on a wide front over the Lüneburg heath—has reached the Elbe south of Hamburg.

The remnants of the Eleventh German Army are defending themselves in the inaccessible terrain of the Harz mountains against the superior forces of the Ninth and First U.S. Armies attacking from the north and west. Both these armies, together with the Third U.S. Army, form the 12th U.S. Army Group of General Bradley.

A relief attack of the XXXIXth German Panzer Corps, with parts of the Panzer Division *Clausewitz*—formed only in March–April from officer cadets of the Panzer Schools and the Labor Service—and the Division *Schlageter* from the southern area of Uelzen pushed through Allied-held territory to the area northeast of Braunschweig where they were confronted by superior enemy forces.

Following the loss of their bridgeheads, first at Wittenberg, then south of Magdeburg the Ninth U.S. Army held out at Barby against fierce attacks by the Twelfth German Army (General Wenck)—a formation also established only in March–April.

To the south, troops of the Twelfth German Army have repulsed the assaults by the First U.S. Army on the bridgehead at Dessau. The right wing of the First U.S. Army, however, had been able to force its way into Bitterfeld and Delitzsch and with elements to advance via Leipzig into the area of Chemnitz–Zwickau.

DÄNEMARK

MÜRWIK
ab 3.5.45

Flensbg.

Schleswg.
Eckernförde

Kiel

Lütjenburg

Neumünster

**March Route and Headquarters
of the OKW from Apr. 20, 1945**

Ostsee

NEUSTADT
2.5.45

SCHLESWIG-HOLSTEIN

Lübeck

Klütz

WISMAR
1.5.45

Rostock

Stralsund

Hamburg

Warin

Schwerin

Sternbg.

Greifswald

MECKLENBURG

POMMERN

Lüneburg

Goldberg

Karow

DOBBIN
30.4.45

Ludwigslust

Malchow

Waren

Elbe

Röbel

Neubrandenburg

Wittenberge

Mirow

**Demarcation line
between east and
west on May 9, 1945**

Rheinsberg

F.A. NEU ROOFEN
24.-29.4.45

Prenzlau

Havelberg

Neu-Ruppin

Fehrbellin

BRANDENBURG

Stendal

Havel

Rathenow

Eberswalde

Nauen

Brandenburg

KRAMPNITZ
23.4.45

BERLIN

Oder

Magdeburg

Elbe

Potsdam

Küstrin

WANNSEE
20.-22.4.45

Dessau

ZOSSEN
bis 20.4.45

Frankft./O.

0 10 20 30 40 50 km

The Third U.S. Army is achieving deep penetrations in the Elster and Fichtel mountains.

In southern Germany—defended by troops of Commander in Chief West, Field Marshal Kesselring—the 6th U.S. Army Group of General Devers (consisting of the Seventh U.S. and First French armies) is taking the offensive.

While making only slow progress around Nuremburg, the Seventh U.S. Army is achieving deep penetrations against the First German Army in the Stuttgart area in the directions of Göppingen and Tübingen.

The First French Army is also pushing south and southeast from the Offenburg–Lahr area against the Nineteenth German Army.

The Russian and Anglo–American forces in Southern and Eastern Europe continue to gain ground against the Army Group Southeast in Yugoslavia (General Löhr) and Army Group Southwest in Italy (General von Vietinghoff).

Parts of the Greek islands are still under German control.

There are no special reports from Norway or Denmark.

On the basis of the events of this day on the various fronts, the following points emerge when estimating the enemies' intentions: The Soviets' main thrust is clearly aimed at Berlin, while their assaults into Saxony and in the Stettin sector are designed to tie down strong German forces with the aim of breaking through our defenses and advancing as far as possible to the west. This is also their aim in the Austria–Bohemia–Moravia area. Here the troops of the Third Ukrainian Front Group mainly have the task of preventing any major German formations from slipping into the Alpine region. The same operational aim motivates the U.S. Command to continue its advance in a southeasterly direction—i.e., towards Austria—with all its strength to link up with the Russian forces.

The Americans are equally determined to render illusory German hopes that effective German forces will be able to set up a defense in the Alps.

The main thrust of the Western Allies under General Bradley is in the center of that front, where the major American forces are committed. Their aim is to join up with the Soviets, thus cutting Germany into two parts, and accelerating the final Allied victory.

The primary aim of the assault of the 21st British Army Group is the capture of the German North Sea harbors with their shipyards and last U-boat bases. The attacks on the lower Elbe point to a breakthrough in the direction of the Baltic.

The German command is trying to stop further withdrawals by its armies. To this end the Commander in Chief Southwest (Italy) receives a timely "Führer Order" to make no further retrograde movements to compensate for local breakthroughs. The withdrawal mentality is to be ruthlessly combatted in all commanders.

In addition, continuation of the withdrawal of the Commander in Chief Southwest (Yugoslavia) to the line from the mouth of the Una to the Save-Virevitica will require prior "Führer Approval." From these instructions, it can clearly be seen how the highest echelon still clings to the fiction of contiguous fronts.

The focal point of all events, however, is the situation within Germany and especially in Berlin.

The Commander in Chief Northwest, Field Marshal Busch, using General Blumentritt's Group, is to stop the enemy thrust on Hamburg by attacking them in their western flank. Our own bridgeheads south of Hamburg are to be held in order to prevent the enemy from interfering with the newly organized Twelfth German Army of General Wenck to their south, in the area west and southwest of Berlin.

The Twelfth Army is still in the throes of organization. Under magnificent leadership, these brave young soldiers have proven to be ready to fight and are still capable of being remotivated in spite of all recent defeats in the Barby–Zerbst–Dessau area. The original task of this army—an attack from east to west in order to relieve Army Group B, trapped in the Ruhr pocket—has been overtaken by the course of events. With its weak forces, it was now to undertake a series of offensive and defensive tasks on two fronts.

On the one hand, the Twelfth Army is to halt the Americans on and east of the Elbe; on the other, it is to keep contact with

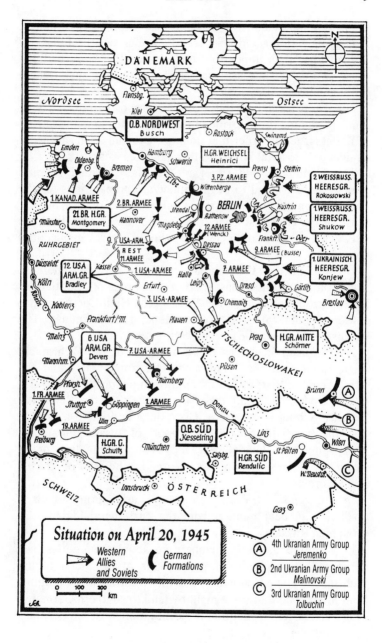

Situation on April 20, 1945

the Seventh German Army in the Mulde–Elbe area and to fight a delaying action against Soviet advance across the Jüterbog–Torgau line. It is impossible for the Twelfth Army to fulfill these two tasks successfully as it does not have the strength for such multiple missions.

Hitler refuses to bow to the alarming reports from all fronts. He is preaching the doctrine of fanatical struggle to the finish. Keitel issues an order that no more German towns are to be designated Hospital Towns as this indicates weakness.

The Commander in Chief of the Navy, Grand Admiral Dönitz, is instructed to begin immediate preparations for the complete mobilization of personnel and material for the defense of the Northern Zone, in case the land communications between north and south Germany should be broken in central Germany.

On the same day, the commander of the La Rochelle defense sector on the Atlantic coast is ordered to break off negotiations for a capitulation (which the Wehrmacht High Command has just heard of) with the French General de Larminat. The defense of La Rochelle is to be continued.

Enemy's action forces the evacuation of the Wehrmacht High Command, the Wehrmacht Operations Staff and the Army General Staff from Zossen toward the north. The Wehrmacht Operations Staff takes up quarters in the Reich Air Defense School at Wannsee. Everything is done in a rush as one can already hear the distant sounds of Russian tank guns.

In Wannsee the headquarters moves into the buildings of the Reich Air Defense School just vacated by the Staff of *Reichsleiter* Bormann.

In the center of Berlin, in sunny early spring weather, civilians can hear gunfire from the east, heralding the approaching Russians.

In Wannsee the staff members go about their duties in a depressed atmosphere. Large sections of the staffs of the Wehrmacht High Command and the Wehrmacht Operations Staff are moved that same night by land to southern Germany. There is a general belief that if the situation in Berlin becomes more critical, continuation of further operations would be directed from southern Germany.

April 21, 1945

The Chief of the Wehrmacht High Command orders the extension of the anti-tank defense lines in *Wehrkreise* [Defense Districts] X (Hamburg), II (Stettin), and III (Berlin). Here, too, defense measures are being ordered at the last moment, when the massive enemy superiority renders them meaningless.

The Twelfth Army is given further detailed instructions from the Wehrmacht Operations Staff concerning its dual task, which from its inception was utterly impossible, i.e. to attack to the west while defending itself in the east.

The Commander in Chief West (Field Marshal Kesselring), who recently relieved Field Marshal von Rundstedt, reports that the First German Army (in the Stuttgart area) believes that it can only regain the initiative by withdrawing to the Swabian Alp. Hitler rejects this decision and orders an offensive solution.

For the first time the Russians fire on the center of Berlin with a long-range gun.

It is strange that in this situation no decision on the final location of the Wehrmacht High Command can be obtained from Hitler. The top echelon still believes a sudden move to southern Germany into the Berchtesgaden area is possible. Numerous headquarters are already there. The only one capable of operating, however, is that section of the Wehrmacht Operations Staff; none of the other sections of the Wehrmacht High Command can function. On orders from the Deputy Chief of the Wehrmacht Operations Staff General Winter, who transferred to southern Germany, they are mostly disbanded and their strength reduced from 1,500 to 400 personnel.

Preparations are made to transfer by air the most essential command organs of the Wehrmacht Operations Staff to southern Germany. Hitler and his close circle may well favor the idea of pulling back into the Alpine Fortress—or the Redoubt, as the enemy calls it—but there exists no Redoubt worthy of the name.

Of course, troops could defend themselves in this area, which is defined by the Allies as extending from the Niederen Tauern in the east, the Dolomites in the south, the Swiss border in the west and the high Bavarian plateau in the north.

A prerequisite for a serious defense of this region, however, would have been its timely occupation, construction of defensive works on all vulnerable entry points and foreseeable critical areas of fighting, as well as stocking it with provisions and building bomb-proof shelters. The entire Alpine area of western Austria and Germany would have to have been converted into a fortress on a grand scale. But no preparations for this contingency were made, and thus a last stand in the Redoubt is out of the question.

The possibility of such a last stand seems to preoccupy the enemy (particularly the Americans) to such an extent that its frustration is one of the main objectives of their operations. The planned transfer of additional staff sections to the Redoubt is overtaken by events occurring the following day.

April 22, 1945

Leading elements of the advancing Red Army have reached the Treuenbrietzen–Zossen line—south of Königswusterhausen to the south of Berlin. Further forces follow these elements in order to exploit the attack. To the east and north of Berlin, the enemy pushes forward to the outer defenses of the capital in heavy fighting.

The Twelfth Army has gained the impression that the Americans are carrying out a "concentration facing a demarcation line" on the Elbe front in the Havelberg area. If this is true, the Americans are going to let the Russians have Berlin as a trophy, even though they could be there first. Meanwhile, there is still no decision as to whether the Twelfth Army should fight with main effort facing east or west. The clear decision should unequivocally be in favor of an attack to the east.

Hitler now decides that he will not go to southern Germany but will take personal control of the struggle for Berlin from the Reich Chancellery.

At 1500 hours, the last survey of the strategic situation takes place in the Reich Chancellery. During this review, Hitler is overcome for the first time by the realization that the war is lost. He accuses his generals and his staff of breach of faith and treachery and talks about taking his own life; but the situation has not yet reached that point. At this time as he decides to stay in Berlin, his closest companions—including Keitel and Jodl—anxious to prove their enduring loyalty to him, offer to stay with him in the Reich Chancellery. He orders Field Marshal Keitel, General Jodl and *Reichsleiter* Bormann to fly to the south to continue directing future operations. All three refuse to follow this order.

Hitler then accepts Jodl's suggestion that the front facing the Anglo–Saxons should be reversed, that all forces employed there should be thrown into the battle for Berlin, and that this operation should be directed by the Wehrmacht High Command itself.

Following this last general review of the strategic situation, the Wehrmacht High Command and the Wehrmacht Operations Staff are transferred to Krampnitz and integrated there into a combined Wehrmacht Command Staff.

In Berlin the situation grows more menacing. The populace still hopes for a miracle from the west. They stand on this Sunday, as on the preceding days, in endless queues outside the grocery stores to get something edible to tide them over the days of the forthcoming siege. From the west, from the direction of Potsdam, hastily assembled, inadequately equipped units are being motorized or issued horse-drawn transport and moved by train, truck or on foot into the defense of Berlin.

Simultaneously, streams of fleeing Berliners are leaving Berlin on all imaginable means of transport. West and northwest of the city, they mix together with columns of refugees, transports of concentration camp inmates and prisoners of war, and members of the Wehrmacht into a massive caravan of aimless, planless humanity, frequently strafed by low-flying fighter aircraft, all trying to save themselves in panic-stricken flight from the Russians toward the west. These are the images of horror that have been seen in the last weeks and months since the enemy crossed the eastern borders of Germany; they cannot be ignored, and their shattering drama increases chaotically from day to day. All these people are trying to save themselves primarily from the indescribable atrocities of the Russians. They are all hoping for some sort of help from the west.

In the evening, Field Marshal Keitel drives to the headquarters of XXth Corps (commanded by General Köhler) in Wiesenburg, southwest of Belzig in Mark Brandenburg, to review the situation there. This corps of the Twelfth Army is formed of three so-called "Young Divisions" and is the only formation half-way capable of effective combat in the entire area west of Berlin. Simultaneous attacks by the IIIrd SS Corps commanded by SS *Obergruppenführer* [Lieutenant General]

Steiner from the north and by the 25th Panzergrenadier Division and the 7th Panzer Division (a remnant formation, scarcely mobile) from the area northwest of Oranienburg against the deep flank of the Russians advancing west on Nauen were designed to ease the pressure on Berlin and, later, to relieve it.

April 23, 1945

The battle for Berlin erupts into full violence on the morning of April 23. Along the Beelitz-Trebbin-Teltow-Dahlewitz line, strong enemy attacks, supported with tanks, are contained. North of the Reich capital, the Soviets are trying to cross the Havel River.

Following his visits to Köhler's corps, Field Marshal Keitel drives to the headquarters of the Twelfth Army in the Alte Hölle forestry station at Wiesenburg, which he reaches at 0100 hours. There he discusses with General Wenck the planned attack on Berlin via Potsdam and the unification of the Twelfth Army with the Ninth Army. The Twelfth Army receives the same instructions directly from the Wehrmacht High Command, with the injunction that strong forces are to be assembled for a thrust on Berlin in a northeasterly direction at the expense of severely reducing the defensive lines on the Elbe and the Mulde. The army has been relieved of its previous, utterly impracticable dual tasks and can now concentrate totally on the "fight against the Soviets."

The same day, reconnaissance and security forces are pushed out to the east and northeast, and combat-effective formations are ordered to prepare to leave their defensive positions that night to operate against the enemy in the east.

At 0600 hours Field Marshal Keitel is at the combat headquarters of the Division *Scharnhorst* (of Köhler's corps) at Kranepuhl, southeast of Belzig. This division just regrouped for an assault on both sides of Treuenbrietzen in the direction of Trebbin, and Keitel has the divisional commander brief him of his plans for this attack. Afterward, he drives back to Krampnitz.

At 1500 hours, Keitel, Jodl and the aides-de-camp go to the Chancellery to review the situation. Here they see Hitler for the last time.

As they return to Krampnitz, immediate relocation of headquarters becomes necessary as the Russians have already crossed the Niederneuendorf Canal, northwest of Spandau, and their tanks are pushing south. It is thus high time to move the headquarters. On April 24, at 0400 hours, after a night march via Nauen (which is reached by enemy tanks one hour later), Neuruppin and Rheinsberg, the headquarters reaches the forestry station of Neuroofen southwest of Fürstenberg.

After his participation in the situation briefing in the Reich Chancellery, Field Marshal Keitel returns to Krampnitz convinced that the operations around Berlin could be positively influenced by his personal efforts; he thus decides to go at once to Twelfth Army headquarters at Seelensdorf, north of Brandenburg, which he reaches at 2300 hours.

Although the day has been dominated by the fighting around Berlin, the Wehrmacht High Command still tries to direct the operations on the other fronts. The Commander in Chief Southwest is advised that the declaration of Pula as a Defensive Region is rescinded. The forces there should be transferred to the protection of Fiume.

The Commander in Chief West receives an operations order for the First and Nineteenth Armies. In accordance with this order, the target is "the recreation of a continuous front in southern Germany, if necessary on the Danube and extending to the Swiss border." Following this, the Commander in Chief West, in a radio message, reports on the combat operations of the Nineteenth Army. This army has been ordered to: "Carry out a breakthrough attack with concentrated forces, or conduct offensive operations throughout the entire combat zone against the rear communications of the enemy. It is particularly important to stop those enemy forces advancing in the area of Stuttgart-Tübingen, in the Black Forest in the direction of Rottweil, and in the Rhine plain south of Lahr."

The Commander in Chief Southwest is granted permission to pull his army group back behind the Tessin and the Po if the penetration of this front cannot be contained. The ultimate aim is to conserve sufficient forces for the defense of the "Blue Line"—a line conceived as running along the southern edge of the Alps.

In addition, a telex arrives from Reich Marshal Göring. In this message, effective 2200 hours April 23, in view of the development of events around Berlin, Göring regards himself as Hitler's successor if no answer to the contrary is received.

Hitler, however, in a radio message, most emphatically forbids the Reich Marshal to undertake any steps in this direction.

April 24, 1945

Against bitter German resistance, the Russians push onward into the area southeast of Brandenburg, south of Potsdam, north of Königswusterhausen and into the outer suburbs east and north of the capital.

Hopes of delaying enemy advances from the south and their encircling movement in the north and northwest depend more and more on the attack by the Twelfth Army west and southwest of Berlin.

At 1945 hours, the Twelfth Army receives orders for the conduct of attack in the battle for Berlin.

At this point, however, the Twelfth Army is no longer capable of forming a solid front facing east; the enemy must be attacked by individual task forces to slow up his advances. The army operations zone is bounded in the north by the Wittstock-Altruppin-Herzberg-Kremmen-Ruppin Canal line. To the south, the zone is delineated by the Dessau-Cottbus general line.

An attack on the entire length of a front of this extent, which has already partially been penetrated by enemy formations, is no longer possible, if only due to lack of forces. A fragmentation of available forces must thus be accepted as inevitable.

To the north the Twelfth Army has contact with the Army Group Vistula, which still retains its name despite the fact that the Vistula (with the exception of the Danzig basin) has been in enemy hands for months. The adjoining Panzer Corps of General Holste, under the Twelfth Army, is totally underequipped and largely immobilized. Only Köhler's corps, on the southern wing, is more or less concentrated and mobile.

The Chief of the Wehrmacht Operations Staff issues a special directive that all available forces are to be concentrated against the deadly Bolshevik enemy; large territorial losses to the Anglo-Americans are to be regarded as being of secondary importance, but the movement of forces from west to east is subject to Wehrmacht High Command permission.

The directive was sent to Commanders in Chief:

West (Field Marshal Kesselring in southern Germany)
Southwest (General von Vietinghoff in Italy)
Center (Field Marshal Schörner in Bohemia and Moravia)
South (General Rendulic in Austria)
Southeast (General Löhr in the northern Balkans)

The night of April 24–25, Hitler signs an order setting up a special Operations Staff B in southern Germany which includes those parts of the Wehrmacht Operations Staff under General Winter which have been transferred there and the command function of the Wehrmacht High Command. In accordance with this order, the Wehrmacht High Command's main function is the continued control of overall operations. In addition the order combines the Wehrmacht Operations Staff and the Army General Staff. This final step, which should have been taken years ago as the only correct organizational measure to achieve meaningful command of overall operations, comes much too late.*

---

*The Eastern Front was under the command of the Army General Staff and formed the only so-called OKH (Army High Command) theater of war, as opposed to the OKW (Armed Forces High Command) theaters. The OKW controlled all other fronts from Norway through Denmark, the western, southwestern to the southeastern fronts. They were subordinate to the Wehrmacht Operations Staff. During the course of the war, the OKW theaters achieved increasing significance and contributed to strengthening the position of the Wehrmacht High Command, and its Wehrmacht Operations Staff, vis-a-vis the Army High Command. There were conflicts of authority, which adversely affected the overall command. Added to this was the fact that Hitler, as Supreme Commander of the Army, was the final arbiter. In controversial decisions between the Wehrmacht Operations Staff and the Army General Staff—such as the transfer of a division from the western to the eastern front—Hitler's instructions had to be sought in every case. The delays which this process entailed often brought with them irreparable damage. Those members of the two headquarters who had the closest contact with Hitler would prevail in enforcing their views.

While Operations Staff B is now inserted as a "branch office" of the Wehrmacht High Command in the defense of the Southern Zone alongside the Commander in Chief West, Field Marshal Kesselring, a Reich Defense Headquarters North under Grand Admiral Dönitz is to be established in the Northern Zone. General Kinzl, heretofore Chief of Staff of the Army Group Vistula, is appointed as Chief of Staff of the headquarters.

Field Marshal Keitel is doing everything possible to spur the Twelfth Army on to greater efforts by visiting them personally. On the evening of April 24, he drives to the XLIst Panzer Corps, the weakest corps on the northern flank of the Twelfth Army. There, in their Panzer Corps headquarters at Klessen, 10 kilometers west of Friesack, he meets with the commander, General Holste, to discuss plans for the impending attack on Berlin.

At this point, General Holste emphasizes his limited mobility due to lack of vehicles. The difficulties for his improvised, hurriedly assembled and motley units owing to the lack of mobility, equipment and weapons are especially serious.

In the current situation, he is in no condition to advance to the east. Keitel regards this as a lack of resolve.

April 25, 1945

The day is dominated by the development of the situation around Berlin. The High Command concentrates on one priority at the expense of all others: the provision of help and relief for the capital. According to incoming reports, every foot of ground around Berlin is being stubbornly contested. Despite this, the Russians push forward to the Babelsberg-Zehlendorf-Neuköln line. Heavy street fighting is taking place in the northern and eastern suburbs. North of Berlin, the outflanking Russian forces reach the area of Nauen and Ketzin with their leading tank units. They have vastly superior forces between Berlin and Holste's corps. Northeast of Oranienburg, the north bank of the Ruppin Canal is still being held against heavy Russian attacks.

In Berlin there remain only the LVIth Panzer Corps of General Weidling, some badly mauled mixed formations and some *Alarm* and *Volkssturm* units. There are only some 50 tanks left.

The defense of the Potsdam area was entrusted to Reymann's corps which consists of two weak divisions, some ad-hoc units, *Alarm* companies and *Volkssturm* units. The clear aim of the Russians—to encircle Berlin—is imminent.

The events of the day in detail:

0030 hours. Radio report from the Twelfth Army. Following withdrawal from the Elbe-Mulde Front the night of April 24–25—and despite a strenuous march—the southern divisions of the Twelfth Army are now (early April 25) in the designated areas facing the Soviets. The Twelfth Army receives approval of its plan to attack from the Niemegk area in the direction of Trebbin with the three battle-worthy divisions of Köhler's corps. By this thrust it is hoped to effect a junction with the Ninth Army which is simultaneously ordered to break out to the west.

Within a couple of hours, however, a violent enemy assault

on a broad front in the area of Treuenbrietzen-Wittenberg against Niemegk has become so heavy that Köhler's XXth Corps has been forced into the defensive in its assembly areas, which they have only just reached.

The Ninth Army also reports steadily increasing pressure by the encircling Soviet army and is involved in bitter defensive fighting. It is questionable if the ordered breakout will succeed. The Wehrmacht High Command issues an order to the Twelfth and Ninth Armies emphasizing the "decisive importance" of the relief operation for Berlin. The order to the Ninth Army states, "The conduct of the Ninth Army is decisive for the success of the operation to cut off those enemy forces which have penetrated Berlin's defensive ring and to free the capital of the Reich, in which the Führer resides, confident of the efforts of his soldiers."

The immediate aim of concentrating the entire Twelfth Army for the assault on Berlin has been rendered impossible by the development of the situation.

Jüterbog falls to the Russians. Köhler's XXth Corps is engaged all day fending off enemy tank attacks.

The city of Potsdam is completely surrounded.

The first juncture between Soviets and Americans takes place at Torgau on the Elbe. Troops of the 58th Guards Division of Marshal Konev's 1st Ukrainian Army Group meet here with men of the 69th U.S. Division of General Bradley's 12th American Army Group.

It seems, however, that the Führer has recovered from the collapse of April 22. He refuses to give up the fight for Berlin. At 1915 hours, we receive a radio message for Grand Admiral Dönitz in Plön/Holstein in which Hitler calls the struggle for Berlin a "fateful German battle." In comparison to this, all other tasks and fronts are of secondary importance. He calls upon the Grand Admiral to support this struggle by moving troops into Berlin by air, land, and water at the expense of any other naval operations.

At 1930 hours, Major Johannmeier (aide-de-camp to the Führer) calls from the Reich Chancellery urgently demanding supplies of ammunition and naval personnel to be flown into Berlin.

At 1940 hours, Field Marshal Keitel has a telephone communication with Steiner's IIIrd SS Corps. He relays the Führer's wish that the attack of the 25th Panzergrenadier Division (with the 7th Panzer Division under command) move forward throught he low-lying bottleneck on Nauen. All available forces should be funneled into this thrust. Keitel states, "It is the express will of the Führer that the nucleus of future operational developments be located here." A personnel and materiel air resupply of Berlin is organized for the night of April 25–26.

To personally emphasize to the troops the significance of the assault to relieve Berlin, General Jodl also drives to the front in the sector of Steiner's corps and the reinforced 25th Panzergrenadier Division.

April 26, 1945

In literal execution of given orders, Field Marshal Keitel and General Jodl dedicate themselves almost exclusively to conducting the Berlin relief operation.

The fighting has intensified there. Violent street fighting is taking place in all suburbs. The enemy is in Zehlendorf, Steglitz and on the southern edge of the Tempelhof field. Fighting is taking place at the Schlesischer and Görlitzer railway stations, and the defending troops, together with the *Volkssturm* and Hitler Youth, are putting up a desperate resistance in the area between Tegel and Siemensstadt.

Fighting has also flared up in Charlottenburg.

At 0025 hours, a telex arrives from the Führer for General Jodl and the Twelfth Army:

> It is most urgently necessary that the relief attacks be speedily executed in the directions ordered. The Twelfth Army is to attack toward the Beelitz-Ferch line and continue east until a junction with the Ninth Army is achieved.
>
> The Ninth Army is to attack toward the west by the shortest route and gain contact with the Twelfth Army. Following the junction of the two armies, the main task is to turn northwards, destroy enemy forces in the southern portion of Berlin and establish a wide corridor of communications with Berlin.
>
> The forward elements of Steiner's assault group advancing northwest of Oranienburg initially must break through to the Bötzow area. The Third Panzer Army of the Army Group Vistula is to conduct its battle to prevent an enlargement of the enemy bridgehead on the west bank of the Oder.

The last point of this order deserves special attention because it states that the primary task of the Third Panzer Army of the Army Group Vistula (Commander in Chief General Heinrici), presently in defensive positions in Mark Brandenburg, Uckermark and Vorpommerm west of the Oder, must be to prevent an extension to the west of the Soviet bridgehead already established on the lower Oder.

For if the Russians should succeed in advancing here, they would threaten the flank and rear of the reinforced 25th Panzergrenadier Division currently advancing on Berlin from the north. On all fronts around Berlin, there are fluid battles in progress with continuous threats to the flank and rear. Simultaneous defense against one side and attack toward another, are common in this confusing battle.

In answer to the Führer's telex received at 0025 hours, General Jodl reports:

> The attack of the Ninth Army has made a promising start. XXth Army Corps hopefully will move the night of April 25–26 in the direction of Beelitz then to swing east and seek to link up with the Ninth Army. Holste's corps is fighting to gain assembly area south of the Havel-Luch area. IIIrd SS Corps has established a bridgehead to the northern edge of Niendorf. Success at Bautzen will allow continuation of attack to north and northwest. Following enemy tank corps attack east of Prenzlau, the Third Panzer Army is stretched to the breaking point. There is imminent danger that the enemy will soon pour into the flank and rear of the forces north of Berlin.
>
> At Lauenburg there is the threat of a strong enemy assault across the Elbe in the direction of Lübeck. To prevent a further split of the north German region in the direction of Lübeck and to get reinforcements to the Third Panzer Army, I suggest concentration in the area southeast of Hamburg of as many troops from the area between the Ems and the Elbe as is technically possible to move by land and sea.
>
> Decision requested.

For days we have been expecting a British assault across the Elbe at Lauenburg. This would help the 21st British Army Group to achieve their goals of reaching the Baltic and cutting Schleswig-Holstein off from northern Germany. We can also expect them to take Hamburg and continue their advance toward Denmark.

The report on the Ninth Army is based on a recent radio

message from that army concerning their starting the breakout as ordered. The word "promising" has, however, been inserted for morale purposes.

The same is true of "Success at Bautzen." It has only local significance and has no operational effect on the overall situation. It is to be seen as a gesture of moral support for Hitler, who apparently is still clinging to the hope that Schörner's army group can break through northwards to relieve Berlin. It remains to be seen whether XXth Corps can attack. Holste's XLIst Corps can no longer be counted on for the assault on Berlin. Due to the Soviet advance west of Berlin, it has only loose contact with the Twelfth Army. The most serious development is in the Third Panzer Army's fighting. By bringing in more troops from the area between the Weser and the Elbe, General Jodl hopes to: 1) reinforce the Third Panzer Army, and 2) transfer more forces to Steiner's IIIrd SS Panzer Corps task force for the assault on Berlin.

At 0815 hours, we receive a radio message from General Krebs in which he confirms that Hitler agrees in principle with General Jodl's proposals.

At 0940 hours, a telex is received from Hitler asking Grand Admiral Dönitz to send everybody who can be spared and armed to help.

The telex continues, "The Führer considers it appropriate to raise the combat-effectiveness of all units by replacing older soldiers of second and third-rate categories with younger sailors and airmen."

At 1145 hours, General Heinrici (Commander in Chief of the Army Group Vistula) asks that the attack of Steiner's task force IIIrd SS Panzer Corps) be cancelled (the assault on Berlin from the area west of Oranienburg) as no success can be expected there and the 25th Panzergrenadier Division and the 7th Panzer Division are needed by the Third Panzer Army in the area of Prenzlau. The request is denied as it runs counter to the Führer's orders for a concentric relief attack on Berlin.

As 1220 hours, we receive a report that the improvement in the mobility of the 7th Panzergrenadier Division, has made insignificant progress due to lack of transport.

General Heinrici is a reliable and perceptive commander-in-chief. He urgently needs the reinforced 25th Panzergrenadier Division on the right wing of his Third Panzer Army to parry a threatening Soviet breakthrough. The success of the thrust on Berlin via Oranienburg as ordered is in reality more than doubtful when one considers the forces available—the 25th Panzergrenadier Division and the 7th Panzer Division task force, which cannot even be given the necessary mobility due to lack of motorized vehicles.

At 1800 hours, the last telephone conversation between General Jodl and the Führer takes place. Following this, Jodl speaks to General Krebs and General Burgdorf who are with Hitler in the Reich Chancellery bunker.

The Führer still hopes that the situation south and southwest of Berlin can be "saved" and thus orders that it is to be made clear to the Ninth Army yet again that it must turn sharply to the north with the Twelfth Army to relieve pressure on Berlin.

At 2030 hours, the following situation report is relayed to Major von Freytag-Loringshoven, aide-de-camp to General Krebs in the Reich Chancellery: "The expansion of the Russian bridgehead in the Army Group Vistula sector is achieving operational significance. Leading enemy tank units are five to six kilometers west of the Randow sector. Counter attack reserves are being concentrated behind the penetration point initially on the Fürstenberg-Neustrelitz-Neubrandenburg line. Twenty-First Army High Command (remnants of General von Tippelskirch's former Fourth Army staff just landed from East Prussia) has been given command of these forces. The attack of the IIIrd SS Corps with the 25th Panzergrenadier Division is in progress. In the Twelfth Army's assault XXth Corps has pushed into the wooded area southwest of Beelitz. The Brandenburg-Plaue road has been blocked by the enemy from the north. Heavy enemy pressure around Rathenow." At 2215 hours, Army Group Vistula submits this situation report: "The leading assault units of the Ninth Army (despite physical separation, this unit belongs to the Army Group) have apparently crossed the Zossen-Baruth road. Considerable losses due to ceaseless enemy air attacks. The enemy is attacking the reinforced 25th Panzergrenadier Division's bridgehead south of the Ruppin Canal with about two divisions. The prospects of a successful continuation of this division's attack appear to the Army Group—on the basis of this new situation—to be even less promising than before. The Randow sector (east of Prenzlau) has been broken through to a depth of six kilometers in some places."

The Army Group Vistula now receives orders by telex for a so-called successful warding off of the enemy breakthrough in the Prenzlau area. Command of this operation is assigned in the newly-organized Twenty-first Army High Command (see Krebs' situation report). This headquarters has no troops at its disposal. However, Grand Admiral Dönitz and the Commander in Chief Northwest, Field Marshal Busch, receive orders to move as many units as the sea transport system will permit from the area between the Weser and the Ems.

General Jodl wishes to block the breakthrough on the Third Panzer Army front without abandoning the so-called relief attack on Oranienburg as General Heinrici had suggested. This appears to be hopeless as moving up new troops is completely unpredictable.

Again on April 26 Field Marshal Keitel is present at the front north of Berlin.

April 27, 1945

Bitter fighting is raging along Berlin's inner defense ring. Despite the overriding problems of controlling the Berlin battle, the Wehrmacht High Command is also making decisions affecting the fighting on other fronts. The Army East Prussia reports that if ammunition resupply does not reach them shortly, then despite all efforts to carry out their duty resistance to the enemy on Kurische Nehrung and in the western area of the Vistula Basin will be broken in a few days.

Despite this and the loss of the coastal fortress of Pillau, the Army East Prussia receives orders to tie down strong enemy forces to permit the resupply of the Army Group Kurland. Therefore, the area around the Putziger Nehrung must continue to be defended.

Meanwhile, another "Führer's Order" arrives. It directs the Assault Group Oranienburg—the reinforced 25th Panzergrenadier Division—to be placed under the command of General Holste's XLIst Panzer Corps near Rathenow and removed from Steiner's command. Apparently Hitler lost confidence in Steiner since he failed to launch his assault on Berlin.

The commander in chief in northern Germany, Grand Admiral Dönitz, visits the headquarters of the Wehrmacht High Command for a briefing and to establish close liaison with an eye to future developments.

In view of the fact that the energy and actions of the highest levels of command are almost exclusively focused on the fight for Berlin, Keitel feels that he must make a "heroic proclamation to the Army Group Vistula and the Ninth and Twelfth Armies, to spur them on to a greater dedicated effort. He says, "The battle for Berlin has reached a culmination and the city can only be saved by the juncture of the Ninth and Twelfth Armies, a 'forceful advance' to the north and a 'breakout' by a reinforced 25th Panzergrenadier Division on Tegel."

On a subsequent visit to Rathenow's combat commander,

Keitel gives him strict orders to hold Rathenow under all circumstances against the Russian advance west of Berlin. Severe measures are to be taken against the troops flooding back out of Rathenow. The units must return to Rathenow. All efforts are to be made to maintain the fiction that General Holste is preparing to advance on Berlin from the Rathenow area. But all of these are acts of desperation destined to have no influence on the overall situation.

At 1500 hours, it becomes irrevocably clear that the enemy has broken through the Third Panzer Army at Prenzlau and is advancing on Lychen-Templin. The Third Panzer Army has no more reserves. As difficult as it is, there is no other decision to make but to abandon temporarily the so-called "Steiner Attack" and to direct the 7th Panzer Division and the 25th Panzergrenadier Division to attack the southern flank of the enemy breakthrough forces in the direction of Templin-Prenzlau.

At 1700 hours, this plan is transmitted as a warning order by telephone to the IIIrd SS Panzer Corps with information copy to the Twelfth Army and the XLIst Panzer Corps.

Following this, a flash priority telex containing the same order is sent to Army Group Vistula and to Twelfth Army Command Headquarters, with information copies to IIIrd SS Panzer Corps and XLIst Panzer Corps. According to this telex, it is still the task of Army Group Vistula to contain the enemy breakthrough and to cover the flanks and rear of the Twelfth Army so that it may continue its assault southwest of Berlin.

The final section of the order states, "The attack west of Oranienburg is to be temporarily halted but the bridgehead is to be retained as a basis for an assault. The 25th Panzergrenadier Division and 7th Panzer Division are to move out of the Templin area to attack the southern flank of the enemy breakthrough."

The highest level of command still refuses to give up Steiner's attack completely and to commit the 25th Panzergrenadier Division and the 7th Panzer Division directly to block the path of the Russian breakthrough force. The Wehrmacht High Command still thinks it possible to stop the Russians with a flanking thrust from the south and then to pull its assault divisions back into the Oranienburg bridgehead.

Despite all the orders and efforts to help Berlin, this day clearly shows that the end of the battle for the capital of the Reich has begun.

An announcement is broadcast over the radio: "Berlin, April 27. Reich Marshal Hermann Göring is ill. For a long time he has been suffering from a chronic heart condition which has now reached an acute stage. Of his own initiative, he has asked to be relieved of his post as commander of the Luftwaffe and all duties that this position entails, at a time which makes extraordinary demands on our energies. The Führer has accepted this request. The new Commander in Chief of the Luftwaffe appointed by the Führer is General Ritter von Greim, who has been simultaneously promoted to Field Marshal."

It is generally accepted that this is the response to Göring's offer to take over power.

April 28, 1945

The inner defense ring of Berlin has been pierced. The relief attempts from the north, west and south, ordered to be mounted by the formations there, have achieved a little success only in the area of the XXth Army Corps of the Twelfth Army.

By means of a surprise attack, this formation has at least succeeded in establishing contact with the Potsdam garrison at the southwestern tip of Lake Schwielow. Thanks to the success of the Twelfth Army, the garrison of Potsdam has been able to fight its way out in small boats and has been saved. This communications corridor is so narrow, however, that it is in constant danger of being cut. There are no forces available to widen the corridor.

At 0130 hours, the Commander in Chief Southwest, General von Vietinghoff, reports that the insurrection in Italy had assumed revolutionary proportions. An opposition government has been formed by the Italian liberation movement.

In the areas of the German Reich which still remain under our control, the fighting intensifies from hour to hour, reaching a climax in the battle for the capital.

At 0300 hours, Field Marshal Keitel speaks by telephone with the Chief of the Army Staff, General Krebs in the Reich Chancellery.

Amazingly enough, despite the fact that the Soviets have occupied almost all of the Berlin area, the telephone communications to the Reich Chancellery remain intact.

The following questions and answers have been reproduced verbatim. During the briefing General Krebs asks: "The Führer is most interested in the attack west of Oranienburg. What is the situation there? Is the attack making progress? The Führer will not accept Steiner as commander. Has Holste taken over command? If we are not relieved within the next 36 to 48 hours, it will be too late."

Keitel's answer: "1) The bridgehead west of Oranienburg

has not yet been sufficiently extended to permit a successful armored assault to be mounted, particularly as the enemy has recognized our intended direction of thrust and is trying to tighten the bridgehead with attacks from three sides.

"2) We had to divert to the east immediately those elements of the 7th Panzer Division which were moving up because enemy tanks have broken through at Templin and were threatening the lines of communication of Steiner's corps; if they continued their thrust they would have succumbed anyway.

"Instead of this, we are moving the Division *Schlageter* from the west into the area northwest of Oranienburg. I shall go to Steiner today and get informed about the extent of the enemy threat from the rear."

Krebs asks: "Why isn't Holste in command there? The Führer has no confidence in Steiner."

Keitel: "Holste is on the west wing of his wide-stretched front, and I haven't been able yet to get him back. At the moment there is nothing to be done there, the way things are."

Krebs: "The Führer expects help by the fastest means. There are only 48 hours at the most, if there is no help by then it will be too late. The Führer stresses this yet again."

Keitel: "We will drive Wenck and Busse on with the utmost urgency. There is a chance of relief by way of a drive to the north."

Busse is the commander of the Ninth Army; we have no information on his breakout attempt.

Telephone communications with the Reich Chancellery were interrupted at 0500 hours.

In the early morning hours the Ninth Army reports: "Breakout attempt failed. Advance armored assault units apparently broke out to the west against express orders or have been destroyed. Other assault group fought to a standstill with heavy losses. The state of morale of officers and men, their physical condition and the low levels of ammunition and fuel will not permit a renewed breakout attempt or a prolonged defense.

"The desperate state of the civilian population, crowded together in the encircled area, is of particular concern.

"It is only the measures taken by all generals which have maintained the discipline of the troops up until now." In conclusion, General Busse, Commander of the Ninth Army, reports, "The Ninth Army will, as a matter of course, maintain its standard of discipline and fight to the end."

The missing armored assault columns, whose breakout was mentioned in the report, did not reach the Twelfth Army and were apparently destroyed by the Soviets. The formulation "apparently broke out to the west against express orders" seems to indicate a realization of the unreliability of even the best units. No soldier wanted to fall into Soviet hands. How indescribably terrible must have been the fate of the civilians, refugees and local inhabitants alike, crushed together like cattle in the smallest of spaces, if it is included in a military report.

Despite this, due to developments in Berlin, a new order is issued by OKW to the Ninth Army, instructing it to break out at once toward the west to join the Twelfth Army.

At 1230 hours, an order arrives from General Krebs in the Reich Chancellery. The order stresses that it remains the task of all combat formations between the Elbe and the Oder to mount concentric attacks to break the encirclement of Berlin with all possible means and at the greatest speed. In light of this decisive mission, the task of repelling those Soviet forces breaking into Mecklenburg is secondary. (Utterly incomprehensible, because if the front of the Third Panzer Army in the Mecklenburg were finally split, the Russians would stand behind Steiner and would destroy him completely.)

At 1238 hours, an order is sent to the Reich Chancellery by radio and to relay orders to the OKW. There is no longer any direct communication with the Reich Chancellery. During the day, General Winter, the Deputy Chief of the Wehrmacht Operations Staff, reports from his location in the south that the Erding transmitter has fallen into the hands of the mutinous commander of the Interpreters Replacement Company and that the appeal of the so-called "Bavarian Liberation Committee" has been broadcast on Radio Munich. The names of Kesselring, Westphal, and other senior public figures have been misused. The content of these appeals is untrue. The most severe counter-measures are being applied.

Field Marshal Keitel returned once more to the formations fighting in the north of Berlin. On this visit he established that the 7th Panzer Division and the 25th Panzergrenadier Division were on the march to Neustrelitz. From this fact, he deduced that the commander in chief of the Army Group Vistula had, on his own account and against the instructions of the OKW, issued orders to abandon the assault on Berlin and the point-less half–measure of a flank attack on the Soviet breakthrough thrust.

On his own initiative he apparently ordered them to block the Soviet breakthrough thrust. In doing this, he seized the only possible course of action which might stop the Soviets and prevent them from overrunning Mecklenburg. Between Neubrandenburg and Neustrelitz, Field Marshal Keitel met General Heinrici and the Commander of the Third Panzer Army, General von Manteuffel. Keitel accused Heinrici of disobedience and sabotaging Hitler's orders. But Heinrici was not intimidated. He committed the 7th Panzer Division (at least those elements which were still combat-effective) south-east of Neustrelitz to hold the enemy breakthrough.

In the meantime, the Ninth Army reports that starting at 1600 hours, the last possible point for air resupply is in the *Platzviereck* drop zone west of Hermsdorf.

In response, General Jodl gives orders that all available aircraft are to be used to resupply this army during the night of April 28–29.

At 1630 hours, telephone communication is restored with General Krebs in the Reich Chancellery. He states that the information sent out in the broadcasts of the Munich-Erding radio station concerning political measures taken by Kessel-ring and Westphal are untrue and are emanating from the commander of the Interpreters Replacement Company, named Gerngross. Most energetic counter-measures have been initi-ated.

1650 hours. Conversation with the Grand Admiral. Grand Admiral's question: "Do we have any knowledge of an enemy report that the *Reichsführer–SS** had made a capitulation offer to the Anglo-Americans and that the reply was that they would only accept a total capitulation which also involved the Soviets?''

Answer: "No knowledge of this news here; investigation under way and, if necessary, counter-declaration will follow."

1720 hours. Telephone report to the *Reichsführer–SS* concerning:

a) the connection and content of General Krebs' message
b) the appeal from Munich-Erding
c) the rumored capitulation offer of the *Reichsführer–SS* and the Anglo-Saxon reply.

In response to this, the *Reichsführer–SS* states that he would inform Grand Admiral Dönitz that this rumor is untrue. He would not broadcast a counter-statement but would prefer to ignore the report.

1830 hours. Order to General Winter to use brutal methods to crush the insurrection in Italy and the conspiracy in the Erding radio station.

1915 hours. Telephone conversation between General Jodl and General Heinrici.

General Heinrici reports that due to the developments in the Neubrandenburg-Friedland area, where some (Soviet) tanks had broken through to south of Anklam, he is forced to pull back his right flank behind the Havel-Voss Canal line to be able to transfer forces to the north. The Division *Schlageter* is to be moved into the area of the Neubrandenburg to slow the enemy drive. General Jodl orders that, since the right wing is not being attacked, it must remain in position, for if it were to fall back more, Wenck's army could no longer be channelled through, toward the north. The Division *Schlageter* must not block the enemy advance elements, but as planned, be as-

---

*[Heinrich Himmler, head of the Gestapo, the Waffen-SS, and Minister of the Interior.]

signed to Steiner's task force. General Heinrici replies that he is unable to follow this order, whereupon General Jodl repeats Field Marshal Keitel's order that the assault force of the XLVIth Panzer Corps is to be used in a northeasterly thrust into the enemy flank.

If Heinrici does not carry out this order, then he personally will have to bear all resulting consequences.

Major of the General Staff Friedel, who had been sent into the area of the IIIrd SS Panzer Corps, reports that the right wing of the Army Group has already moved behind the Havel-Voss Canal in the Liebenwalde-Zehdenick line and that only weak elements are in action in the western part of the Schorfheide.

This is another proof of the commander's unauthorized action.

In south Germany, the Operations Staff B, General Winter and Commander in Chief West are ordered that as soon as the Americans stop advancing or give up terrain, they are to transfer these forces to the eastern front immediately.

The operations staff, army groups and armies are directed to suppress rumors. A continuous exchange of information must foster the sense of constant and close contact with the Supreme Command.

It is stressed that only the orders of Supreme Command are to be obeyed to the letter and carried out to the last.

2302 hours. Radio message to the western fortresses: The Führer is still thinking of them and expects that they will continue to carry out their duty in the same exemplary, soldierly manner that they have already displayed. Any independent initiative is forbidden.

2330 hours. General Heinrici, Commander in Chief of the Army Group Vistula, and his chief of staff, Brigadier General von Trotha, are removed from their posts by Field Marshal Keitel in response to their refusal to obey orders. They are replaced by General Student and Brigadier General Dethleffsen.

April 29, 1945

Night and day April 29, house to house fighting rages in the center of Berlin.

At 0300 hours, General Jodl demands immediate report from the Deputy Chief of Wehrmacht Operations Staff, General Winter, concerning the mutineers who had broadcast the appeal of the Bavarian Liberation Committee on the Erding transmitter. At 0340 General Winter reports that Radio Munich was reporting the news of Hitler's death.

0510 hours. General Winter is informed that this report is false and that at this time telephone communications with the Reich Chancellery are still being maintained. General Jodl expects that the measures ordered to be taken against the gang of traitors in Erding will be carried out.

0735 hours. General Winter reports on the situation in Munich: "Ritter von Epp's attitude is unclear. The mutinous commander of the Interpreters Company has escaped with his officers. The effects of these Munich broadcasts on front line troops can occasionally be observed. Most energetic counter-measures assured."

1100 hours. The Grand Admiral reports that the enemy has established a bridgehead over the Elbe at Lauenburg.

1235 hours. Last conversation with Berlin (with Combat Commandant General Weidling, no longer with the Reich Chancellery.

1237 hours. General Heinrici (now relieved of command) reports that he has asked General von Manteuffel to assume temporary command of Army Group Vistula. General von Manteuffel reports that in this critical and decisive hour he cannot relinquish command over his Third Panzer Army. In response Field Marshal Keitel orders Lieutenant General von Tippelskirch to assume command of the Army Group at once.

General von Tippelskirch, who initially also was reluctant to take over this command, was most urgently reminded where his true duty lay, according to Keitel's own account. Following this he agreed to assume command of the Army Group in this desperate situation. Keitel said, "Tippelskirch understood the situation and promised to throw himself fully into his task."

1250 hours. The balloon radio aerial at Fürstenberg has been shot down by enemy aircraft.

1600 hours. Situation report by radio to the Reich Chancellery: "No report from the Ninth Army; Twelfth Army continues to press on to Berlin via Potsdam. Left wing of Twelfth Army and right wing of Army Group Vistula in successful defense. Army Group Vistula will try to bring the enemy breakthrough to a halt on the line running through Liebenwalde–Lychen–Neubrandenburg–Anklam–Usedom–Wollin."

The headquarters of the OKW is now so threatened by the enemy advance that at 1900 hours it moves through the woods to Dobbin, east of Krakow in south Mecklenburg. Its stay there is limited to one day owing to further rapid Soviet advance to the west.

1931 hours. Received radio message from General Krebs and *Reichsleiter* Bormann for Field Marshal Keitel: "Foreign press is broadcasting new treachery. The Führer expects that you react with utmost speed and ruthlessness. Wenck, Schörner and others are expected to prove their loyalty to him by most rapid relief."

2028 hours. Telex to Army Group Vistula with earlier oral transmission: "It is the task of Army Group Vistula to hold the south and east front and to concentrate all available forces to attack and smash the enemy breakthrough in the direction of Neubrandenburg."

2300 hours. In Dobbin General Jodl receives the following radio message from the Führer: "Report to me immediately:

1. Where are Wenck's advance elements?
2. When will they continue to attack?

3. Where is the Ninth Army?
4. In which direction will the Ninth Army break through?
5. Where are Holste's points?''

It seems that the Reich Chancellery still expects to be relieved. However, this hope finally has to be buried in light of the latest events and a situation report from the Twelfth Army received at 2300 hours:

> The army and, in particular XXth Corps (which was temporarily able to establish communications with the Potsdam garrison) has been forced into the defensive along the whole front so that a further assault on Berlin is no longer possible, particularly as we can no longer rely on the effective armed strength of the Ninth Army.
>
> The deep flank and rear of the army is being threatened by the American advance on Coswig west of Wittenberg on the Elbe. Due to the American advance and to the stiff resistance and counter-attacks of the Soviets, the impossibility of mounting a further attack to the north is growing considerably. Additionally, American activity today along the heights of the Elbe makes it appear likely that they will soon attack the whole German western front. In view of this, the army requests an immediate decision as to its further combat tasks.

The decision is as follows: "To Twelfth Army High Command: If the Commander in Chief of the Twelfth Army is convinced that it is no longer possible to press on with the advance on Berlin due to full knowledge of the state of the XXth Corps, and despite the realization of the high moral and historical responsibility that we bear, preparations are to be made for the XXth Corps to break out northward over the lower Havel. Report your reaction to this. Orders for the execution of this plan will be issued from here while submitting it simultaneously to the Führer. Signed Keitel."

At about midnight an order is issued to move forces from the area between the Ems and the Elbe to an area east of Hamburg due to a threatened British advance from their bridgehead at Lauenburg. The Russians continue to advance and attack from east to west in Mark Brandenburg and in Mecklenburg.

A letter from General Winter reaches General Jodl requesting advance information as to Hitler's successor should the Führer be killed. It has obviously been accepted in the southern theater that the situation in Berlin is hopeless.

In Kurland and the Vistula plain, the German forces have been able to repel all Soviet attacks. Only on the Frische Nehrung have the Soviets been able to gain a foothold.

Following the juncture of the Russian and American forces at the Elbe, the struggle continues in the two German combat zones in the north and in the south. The course of the front is delineated by two powerful defense lines as follows:

In the north: from the lower Ems through Bremen to Hamburg, along the Elbe to the area of Havelberg, along the Rhine, the Hohenzollern Canal and over the eastern fringe of the Mecklenburg lake district to the Stettin Haff.

In the south: from Lake Constance along the northern foothills of the Alps and the Danube to the area of Bavarian Forest and the Bohemian Forest, the Saxon mountain range and the northern edge of the Sudetenland to the Moravian Basin at Troppau. From here it continues through the Beskid Mountains and White Carpathians via Brünn to the eastern edge of the Alps.

Bitter fighting continues in the Brandenburg-Berlin area and in the Saxon-Bohemia border area.

Fortress Breslau also repels Soviet attacks.

German forces are still defending Fortress Holland and the Atlantic fortresses at St. Nazaire and Lorient.

In northern Italy, German forces are trying to stop the Allied troops that have broken through at a series of blocking positions.

0030 hours. Army Group Vistula receives orders to assume immediate command of the Twelfth Army, which has already been ordered to attack to the north.

The Twelfth Army's task is to assault northwards with the XXth Army Corps and to join up with XLIst Panzer Corps (Holste) north of the main Havel canal. The center of Berlin is still being held in bitter house-to-house fighting.

0100 hours: After much deliberation, Field Marshal Keitel replies to the Führer's verbal instructions of yesterday as follows:

"1. Wenck's forward elements are bogged down south of Lake Schwielow.
2. The army, therefore, cannot continue its attack on Berlin.
3. The bulk of the Ninth Army has been encircled.
4. Holste's corps has been forced into the defensive."

Following a report by General Winter on the situation in Fortress Breslau, there is a radio message to Winter saying that a breakout attempt from Breslau may be made if there is a slight chance of success and if forces of Army Group Center can help from outside.

There are no further requests for situation reports from the Führer's bunker; neither are any further significant military instructions issuing from there. Signal communication is, however, maintained with the bunker to keep up the impression that Hitler can still influence military operations.

German forces are still fighting in their last footholds in East Prussia, with their main effort concentrated on Hela and in the Vistula delta. The OKW approves the conduct of operations reported by Army High Command East Prussia. Main point of defense continues to be Hela.

The deterioration of the situation of Army Group Vistula caused by relentless and repeated attacks by the Russians, forces the OKW to adopt measures which are aimed at holding the front there at the eleventh hour.

For this purpose, five staff officers of the Defense Staff are sent off to carry an order to all commanders on the northern front of Army Group Vistula, instructing them to hold their present position at all costs. They are to explain this order and the fact that it is only by holding the enemy in the Mecklenburg lake district, regardless of the cost involved, that the Twelfth Army can be saved from the Potsdam-Belzig-Brandenburg area.

Field Marshal Keitel appeals personally and most urgently "to the conscience and sense of honor of all commanders" to carry out "their duty to their comrades" in this situation.

Due to the "too late" order to break off a desperate and pointless relief attempt, this army, which had fought with exemplary bravery, was itself now in danger of being destroyed by superior Soviet forces.

1600 hours. General Winter is informed of the situation in the Northern Zone and is ordered to concentrate his defenses into a coherent ring with its strongest force towards the east to preserve all possible areas from Bolshevism. General Jodl: "The fight must go on to gain time for political advantage."

This "time for political advantage" refers to an attempt to split the Soviets from their Western Allies. The hope is that if this division can be achieved, there may yet be an upturn in Germany's fortunes, even at this late stage.

1900 hours: Another situation report is sent by radio to General Krebs in the Reich Chancellery.

According to this report, the situation of Army Group Center and of Army Group South, which were both on the defensive against the Red Army, have stabilized.

The Army Group Southeast is conducting an orderly withdrawal to the Fiume-Varazdin line.

In Army Group Southwest, the Fourteenth Army in upper Italy has been largely destroyed; the Tenth Army is withdrawing behind the Etsch.

The Americans have penetrated into southern Bavaria.

The British have established a bridgehead at Lauenburg.

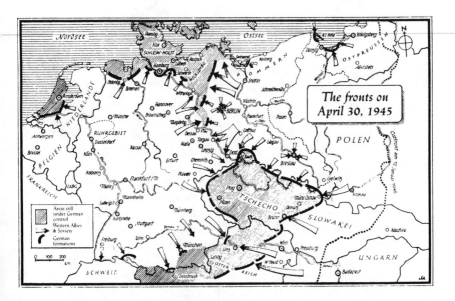

The fronts on
April 30, 1945

This was the situation when, at 1935 hours, a report arrived from Army Group Vistula:

"Enemy has entered Malchin in Mecklenburg with 40 tanks. Broken through at Demmin to the west. XLVIth Panzer Corps has at once been withdrawn into the defile between the Kölpin and Malchow lakes. The 25th Panzergrenadier Division is pushing north to destroy the enemy advancing west from the Demmin area."

2215 hours: Phone call from Lieutenant Commander Lüdde-Neurath (aide-de-camp of Grand Admiral Dönitz) to Lieutenant Colonel of the General Staff Brudermüller (aide-de-camp of General Jodl): "Field Marshal Keitel and General Jodl are requested to come at once to the Grand Admiral and to bring with them all files on the conduct of military operations. The Führer has nominated the Grand Admiral as his successor."

This message was sent by radio. "Advise when Field Marshal Keitel and General Jodl will arrive."

The above-mentioned radio message concerning Hitler's successor reached the Grand Admiral from Berlin at 1835 hours in the following form:

Grand Admiral Dönitz,
    In place of former Reich Marshal Göring, the Führer appoints you to be his successor. Written authorization follows. Effective immediately, you are to take all measures required by the present situation.

Bormann.

It now seems almost certain that the fate of Hitler and his close associates in the Reich Chancellery is sealed; otherwise a radio message in this form would not have been sent. The top echelon doubts whether Hitler is still among the living.

May 1, 1945

In the center of Berlin, the brave garrison is defending itself from a very limited area against superior Bolshevik forces. South of the Reich capital, some formations of the Ninth Army have been able, by some as yet unexplained means, to join up with Wenck's Twelfth Army after all, and are currently engaged in a heavy defensive battle with Soviet forces on the Niemegk–Beelitz–Werder line. According to other reports, the Twelfth Army has only been able to rescue remnants of the Ninth Army. Our troops are fending off heavy enemy attacks between Rathenow and Fehrbellin.

In Mecklenburg the main Bolshevik thrust is aimed at the area between Müritz and Demmin. Part of the enemy forces have turned off to the northeast and are trying to vain to cross the Peene defile east of Anklam.

In northwestern Germany, the center of gravity of fighting lay in the Bremervörde–Stade area. There was heavy fighting in the enemy bridgehead at Lauenburg. South of Boitzenburg the enemy has managed to land on the north bank of the Elbe.

American armored formations have broken out of the Bavarian Forest and bypassed Passau, reaching the Danube east of that town. In Upper Bavaria the enemy is advancing southward from Regensburg. Enemy forces have forced their way into Munich. The enemy has reached Garmisch–Partenkirchen from the Allgäu and is advancing on Mittenwald.

In upper Italy, our divisions are fighting their way northward, defending themselves against continuing attacks by superior enemy forces. They have destroyed communist terrorist groups which sought to cut off their withdrawal.

The defenders of Breslau have repelled Bolshevik attacks.

In answer to the radio message signed by Bormann and received the previous evening, Grand Admiral Dönitz sends the following radio message to the Führer at 0122 hours.

My Führer:
My loyalty to you will be unconditional. I shall continue to
make all efforts to relieve you in Berlin. If fate nevertheless
compels me to rule the Reich as your appointed successor, I
shall continue this war to an end worthy of the unique, heroic
struggle of the German people.

Grand Admiral Dönitz

At this time, the Grand Admiral is in his headquarters in
Plön in Holstein. Senior staffs no longer essential for the
conduct of operations have been concentrated there.

At 0430 hours, the OKW Headquarters and attached headquarters leave Dobbin, which is under threat of Soviet attack,
and move to Wismar in Mecklenburg.

There, at 1040 hours, a radio message is received from SS
Gruppenführer [Major General] Kaltenbrunner reporting the
collapse of the Italian front.

At 1053 hours, Grand Admiral Dönitz in Plön receives the
following radio message from *Reichsleiter* Bormann:

Testament is in force. I will join you as soon as possible. Until
then, I recommend that publication be delayed.

Bormann

This is the original text of the radio message confirming the
news of Hitler's death.

As the circumstances in the Reich Chancellery cannot be
established, and as it cannot be confirmed if this reported
death is based on facts, Dönitz orders by radio that witnesses
in Plön and the Reich Chancellery (including the radio opera-
tors) should be interrogated by military courts, presided over
by military judges and their statements made evidence. This
examination confirms—if only by radio—that Hitler is dead.
In view of the events in Berlin and in the Reich Chancellery,
there can no longer be any doubt that Hitler is dead.

Dönitz—his successor—receives a difficult inheritance.

At 2203 hours that evening, the German Broadcasting Company transmits the following message:

"Our Führer, Adolf Hitler, fighting to the last breath against Bolshevism, fell for Germany this afternoon in his operational headquarters in the Reich Chancellery. On April 30 the Führer appointed Grand Admiral Dönitz his successor."

Following the broadcast announcement of the Führer's death, Grand Admiral Dönitz addressed the German people:

German men and women, soldiers of the German Wehrmacht. Our Führer, Adolf Hitler, has fallen. The German people bow in deepest mourning and reverence. He foresaw at an early stage the dreadful danger of Bolshevism and dedicated his existence to the struggle against it.

At the end of this, his fight, and his unerringly undeviating life, comes his heroic death in the capital of the German Reich. His life was dedicated solely to Germany. His efforts in the struggle against the Bolshevik storm flood extended also for Europe and the entire civilized world.

The Führer has appointed me to be his successor.

I assume the leadership of the German people in this fateful hour fully conscious of the burden of responsibility. It is my first duty to save Germany from destruction by the advancing Bolshevik enemy. For this aim alone the military struggle continues. As far and as long as the British and Americans hinder the achievement of this aim, we shall be forced to continue to fight and to defend ourselves against them as well.

Under these circumstances, the Anglo–Americans are no longer fighting for their own peoples but solely for the spreading of Bolshevism in Europe.

The efforts of the German people both in the struggles on the battlefields and in the suffering on the home front are unique in history. In the time of need which lies before our people, I will do everything in my power to create bearable living conditions for our brave men, women and children.

In all this I need your help. Give me your trust, because your path is also my path. Uphold order and discipline in town and country, let each do his duty at his post. Only in this way will we be able to minimize the suffering that the coming period will bring to each and every one of us, and prevent the collapse. If we do what is within our power, the Lord God will not forsake us after so much suffering and sacrifice.

Following his address to the German people, Grand Admiral Dönitz issued the following order of the day to the German Wehrmacht:

German Wehrmacht! My comrades! The Führer has fallen. True to his great concept of protecting the people of Europe from Bolshevism, he put his life on the line and died a hero's death. With him one of the greatest heroes of German history is gone. In proud reverence and mourning we lower our banners before him.

The Führer has appointed me to be his successor as head of state and as Supreme Commander of the Wehrmacht. I assume command of all services of the German Wehrmacht with the desire to continue the fight against the Bolsheviks until the fighting troops and the hundreds of thousands of families of the eastern German region have been saved from enslavement or destruction.

I must continue the fight against the British and the Americans for as long as they try to impede my struggle against the Bolsheviks.

The situation demands from you, who have already achieved such great historic deeds, and who are now longing for the end of the war, further unconditional dedication. I demand discipline and obedience. Only by absolute obedience of my orders will chaos and destruction be avoided. Anyone who evades his duty now, and thus condemns German women and children to death or enslavement, is a coward and a traitor.

The oath of allegiance which each of you swore to the Führer is now absolutely transferred to me as the Führer's appointed successor. German soldiers, do your duty. The life of our nation depends upon it!

Grand Admiral Dönitz continues to command through the OKW staff and its associated staffs and retains Keitel and Jodl in their positions. He discusses all pending issues with both of them. Keitel and Jodl return temporarily to headquarters (which has now been moved from Wismar to Neustadt in Holstein), only to move two days later to Flensburg–Mürwik to be with the Grand Admiral.

In the German Northern Zone there remain only the following command staffs: In the northwest the Commander in Chief Northwest, Field Marshal Busch, and in the east the Army Group Vistula of General Student.

General Dethleffsen, chief of staff of this Army Group, writes to General Jodl of a "type of disintegration among the troops." This symptom is only too understandable as the fighting can achieve no success having anything more than a local significance.

Hitler is dead and every German is understandably striving for only one thing in these last hours of the war—to avoid falling into Russian hands. So it happens that entire formations of combat troops, individual soldiers, groups and headquarters of all Wehrmacht services and para-military organizations, often on their own initiative, decide to leave the Brandenburg– Mecklenburg area and withdraw toward the lower Elbe, Hamburg and Schleswig–Holstein.

May 2, 1945

Wehrmacht Bulletin:

"The Führer has fallen at the head of the heroic defenders of the Reich capital. He sacrificed his life dedicated to defend his people and Europe from destruction by Bolshevism. This example of 'faithful unto death' is binding for all soldiers.

"The remnants of the brave garrison of Berlin, split up into individual combat groups, fight on in the governmental area of the city."

From Field Marshal Kesselring (commander in chief of the entire southern theater) a report that the Commander in Chief Southwest, in view of tactical and political developments in Italy, has concluded a cease-fire agreement with Field Marshal Alexander. It should come into effect at 1200 hours, May 2, 1945.

The senior leadership has now accepted the general tendency which has become common today: "The rescue of as many Germans as possible from Soviet clutches and the opening of negotiations with the Western Allies."

A radio message to this effect is sent to the Army Group Vistula:

"The battle is to be conducted so that as many formations of the Army Group as possible can fight their way in an organized fashion into the British and American dominated areas west of the Dömitz–Wismar line. Local negotiating possibilities with British and American commanders may be pursued. Commander in Chief Northwest is fighting a delaying action to win time for negotiations between the OKW and the British over the northwestern German Zone."

To prepare the way for the capitulation of the Northern Zone, the OKW sends a telephone order evening of May 2, 1945 to the Combat Commandant Hamburg, Commander in Chief Northwest and *Gauleiter* Kaufmann:

1. It is not intended to defend Hamburg, in order to preserve the city and population from total destruction.

2. It will therefore be necessary to send an emissary at 0800 hours on May 3, who will have the authority to negotiate that:

a) Hamburg will not be defended.

b) German forces will withdraw over the Elbe without a fight.

The advance announcement of these emissaries will be made today. Simultaneous with this emissary, a delegation from the OKW will be sent, and this is also to be announced in advance today. It consists of two admirals and a general officer with aides in four vehicles.

The delegation has the mission of clarifying wider-ranging questions.

Confirmation of the willingness of the Commander in Chief of the 21st British Army Group to receive this delegation in the morning of 3 May and notification regarding the location of the rendezvous is to be accomplished.

Keitel

Field Marshal

During the course of the morning, General Dethleffsen phones in a report that American tanks have appeared before Schwerin. Rostock has been occupied by the Russians. Army Group Vistula reports that it intends to break out of the Ludwigslust–Parchim area if the Americans try to hinder them in their operations against the Bolsheviks.

At 1300 hours, General Jodl drives to Plön to review the situation with the Grand Admiral.

At 1300 hours, a situation report is passed to General Winter in the Southern Zone notifying him that after receiving a British offer to spare the city of Hamburg, a delegation from the OKW led by Admiral von Friedeburg (Commander in Chief of the Navy) would be sent on May 3 to discuss wider-ranging questions with the Commander in Chief of the 21st British Army, Field Marshal Montgomery.

Points for discussion with Montgomery:

The aim is to save as many German soldiers and Europeans from enslavement and bolshevization. Thus, the withdrawal of

Army Group Vistula into the Zone under control of the Anglo–Saxons. Protection of those people in the Schleswig–Holstein area from destruction and starvation. Supply of medical supplies into this area. Preservation of the larger communities from destruction by bombardment. In addition, means to protect central and northern Europe from further chaos. Authority of Admiral von Friedeburg.

General Blaskowitz, Commander in Chief Holland, reports that negotiations have been successfully completed with Allied supreme command to relieve the food supply crisis for the civilian population in Holland.*

General Field Marshal Busch has been made responsible for conduct of operations in the Northern Zone, excluding Norway and Denmark, and has been appointed Commander in Chief North by the Grand Admiral.

---

*After the Allies surrounded the areas still under German occupation, conditions for the Dutch civilian population continued to deteriorate. The food crisis was much improved by the delivery of supplies permitted by the Allies who, after negotiations with the German military authorities, declared that they would be willing to halt along the "Grebbe Line." For their part, the Germans agreed not to flood any further areas and to halt acts of repression against the Dutch.

The Allies apparently thought that Fortress Holland would fall into their hands sooner or later in the wake of the general German capitulation.

May 3, 1945

Remnants of the Berlin garrison are still putting up resistance in the capital of the Reich.

In the early afternoon, the OKW staff is moved from Neustadt in Holstein to Flensburg–Mürwik, in direct proximity to the new head of state, Grand Admiral Dönitz. Field Marshal Keitel and General Jodl drove to Mürwik at 0400 hours this morning.

At 1000 hours a review of the strategic situation takes place with the Grand Admiral. At 1120 hours the Combat Commandant Schleswig receives orders to concentrate all available forces on the Kaiser Wilhelm Canal which is to be defended. These orders should be regarded as precautionary measures, as it is not yet clear how negotiations with Field Marshal Montgomery will go. No one actually believes that the canal sector will be defended. This can be deduced from the paragraph of the orders which forbids destruction of the canal bridges. This paragraph has been inserted at the Grand Admiral's express wish.

At midday there is a conference with *Gauleiter* Terboven from Oslo and the Commander in Chief Norway, General Böhme.

The outcome of the conference is sent to Army High Command Norway in a telex which states that the Commander in Chief Norway, in his capacity as military district commander, is empowered to issue orders as he sees fit to all Wehrmacht services and other organizations except the police.

Lieutenant Colonel of the General Staff de Maizière flies to Kurland and East Prussia to explain personally the Grand Admiral's aims and the arrangements for evacuating the troops there.

At 1453 hours, there is a radio message addressed to Field Marshal Kesselring and General Winter: "Field Marshal Kesselring is authorized to conclude an armistice with the 6th

American Army Group for all troops on the western front between the Böhmerwald and the upper Inn. The negotiations must establish how far to the east the Anglo–Americans intend to advance. The negotiations must form the basis for the rescue of the Army Groups Löhr, Rendulic and Schörner. The Seventh Army is to be placed under Schörner's command.''

At 1930 hours, there is a radio message to the Army East Prussia and the Army Group Kurland:

> The changed military situation in the Reich calls for the accelerated evacuation of numerous military units out of the East and West Prussian areas, as well as out of Kurland. The combat operations of the Army East Prussia and the Army Group Kurland are to achieve this aim.
>
> Personnel of the returning units are to embark equipped with the light infantry weapons. All other materiel, including horses, is to be left behind and destroyed.
>
> Army Group Kurland is given operational freedom to pull back the main front line into the advance bridgeheads around the ports of Libau and Windau.
>
> The Navy will send all available transport capacity to East Prussia and to Kurland.

The decisive event of the day is the opening of communications between the German emissary Admiral von Friedeburg and Field Marshal Montgomery. With this step, at least the hope of concluding an armistice with the British becomes a real possibility.

The turn of events in the Southern Zone also forces Field Marshal Kesselring to make immediate use of similar possibilities to save what can be saved.

May 4, 1945

Last report on Berlin: "The battle for the capital of the Reich is over. In a unique, heroic struggle, troops from all services of the Wehrmacht and units of the *Volkssturm* resisted to the last breath, true to their oaths of allegiance, and have given an example of the best traditional German military values."

At 0925 hours, Wehrmacht command sends a signal to the commandant of the island of Rügen, instructing him not to defend against the Russians. He is to evacuate as many people as possible and then hand the island over to the Soviets.

Admiral von Friedeburg is still negotiating with the Field Marshal Montgomery, commander in chief of the 21st British Army Group. Von Friedeburg is offering the capitulation of the Third Panzer, the Twelfth and Twenty-first Armies and all forces in the German Northern Zone. He will request permission to withdraw through Allied lines those troops currently fighting the Soviets so that they will not have to capitulate to the Russians. After Field Marshal Montgomery refuses to conclude capitulation with the Germans on this basis, the negotiations are eventually brought to a positive conclusion when Montgomery lets von Friedeburg know that all soldiers who give themselves up individually could be taken into British captivity. It is agreed that the armistice will take effect in the German Northern Zone starting at 0800 hours, German Summer Time, on May 5, 1945. On hearing this, the Grand Admiral decides to extend the agreement with Montgomery to the entire Northern Zone and to push ahead with it. General Jodl makes a proposal not to give up the trump cards of Norway and Heligoland yet.

Meanwhile, the struggle against the Soviets continues with unabated fury.

Thus at 0930 hours, the Army High Command East Prussia

receives a radio message giving approval for continued combat operations from the Hela sector.

The fighting against the British 21st Army Group, however, has not ended on this May 4, since the armistice will not come into effect until May 5. Thus General Hoffman, who has been appointed commander of the Kaiser Wilhelm Canal defense zone, receives a briefing on the situation from General Jodl in which he is informed that the Grand Admiral intends to occupy and possibly defend the Kaiser Wilhelm Canal.

The rumors currently circulating, especially those provoked by the Grand Admiral's proclamation to the German people and Wehrmacht of May 2, have given rise in military headquarters to the impression that all resistance is to be ended. Thus at 1120 hours an order is transmitted that the battalion of the 264th Infantry Division, disarmed the previous day by the Kiel Naval Headquarters, is at once to be given back all its weapons and is to be sent to Holtenau to go into action.

The order states: "The war is not yet over today. The Grand Admiral's military orders are the only ones that are valid. The Kaiser Wilhelm Canal is to be defended. All forces are to be concentrated there. Exception: Flensburg (open city); all other rumors are false. Those who are circulating rumors are to be opposed."

At 1130 hours, a telex is sent to Armed Forces Commander Norway and Denmark: "Grand Admiral wishes to avoid incidents which could aggravate the situation with Western foes."

At 1400 hours, the Grand Admiral states that he wishes orders to be sent to the U-boats to undertake no further offensive actions for the time being and to head for home unobserved.

Considerations have also been given to the final seat of the main military headquarters and the Reich government, based on the assumption that the best location would be within the largest contiguous area under our control. The most appropriate location to fulfill these requirements would be Prague. Due to current developments, however, this idea is dropped.

The following report contains details of the negotiations which took place between Field Marshal Montgomery and the

OKW delegation in the tactical headquarters of the 21st British Army Group:

Montgomery's Proposals and Demands:
1. All members of the German armed forces who come into the 21st Army Group area from the east and wish to surrender will be treated as prisoners of war. The 21st Army Group can not make an exception for the surrender of an entire German army which is fighting against the Russians.
2. A discussion regarding the civilian population is not necessary.
3. Field Marshal Montgomery demands that all German forces in Holland, Friesland (including the islands and Heligoland), Schleswig and Denmark, lay down their weapons and surrender to him unconditionally.
4. As soon as the surrender has been agreed upon, he is prepared to discuss the form of occupation of these areas, the treatment of the civilian population, etc. Admiral von Friedeburg has no authority to agree to a surrender as formulated in paragraph 3. Friedeburg therefore wishes to send two officers, Rear Admiral Wagner and Major of the General Staff Friedel, to the Armed Forces High Command to obtain approval and bring it back.

   He requests that Field Marshal Montgomery make a plane available as road movements are too slow and also asks that Admiral von Friedeburg and General Kinzl may in the mean time remain in Field Marshal Montgomery's headquarters.

That was the report.

Later the negotiations are resolved in accordance with Montgomery's demands.

General Eisenhower is informed that Grand Admiral Dönitz wishes to send Admiral von Friedeburg—who has just concluded negotiations with Montgomery—to his headquarters.

At 2230 hours, the following telex is sent: "Armed Forces Commander Denmark is authorized to declare Copenhagen an open city in case of attack."

At 2300 hours, a radio message is sent to Operations Staff B and Army Group Center informing Field Marshal Kesselring that, after the completed capitulation, he, as Commander in Chief South, with Operations Staff B, is to assume command of the Army Groups Center, South and Southeast. The fighting is to be conducted to win time to save as much of the German populace from the Soviets as possible.

The start of the armistice at 0800 hours on May 5, 1945 includes the cessation of all naval traffic out of the Norwegian and Dutch regions. All air movement in the areas controlled by Commander in Chief North and Armed Forces Commander Denmark is to cease at the same time.

The decisive result of this tense May 4 is the final conclusion of the armistice with the British for those elements of the German Wehrmacht stationed in the Northern Zone, which becomes effective on May 5, 1945.

May 5, 1945

In accordance with the agreement reached with the Commander in Chief of the British Army Group, Field Marshal Montgomery, firing has ceased since 0800 hours in Holland, northwestern Germany from the Ems estuary to the Kieler–Förde and in Denmark, including offshore islands.

The ceasefire also affects the operations against the British by the navy and the merchant marine out of and into the ports of the above-mentioned areas. After almost six years of honorable combat, Grand Admiral Dönitz agreed to this armistice because the war against the Western powers makes no more sense and is only leading to the loss of precious German blood, particularly through the bombing raids.

Resistance against the Soviets continues, however, in order to save as many Germans as possible from the Bolshevik terror.

All forces of the German Wehrmacht not affected by the armistice carry on fighting against all attackers.

The Atlantic coastal fortresses report reconnaissance and artillery activity. In Holstein the enemy occupies Kiel.

At 0028 hours, General Kinzl, who has remained with Field Marshal Montgomery as liaison officer, reports, "A British airborne force consisting of transport planes with fighter escort will land in Copenhagen on May 5. Ensure that flight and landing will be unimpeded."

Various questions concerning the armistice remain to be clarified.

The Grand Admiral wishes that no demolitions or scuttling of ships be undertaken. The British airborne landing will be secured as wished.

At 0042 hours, General Kinzl requests the dispatch of authorized Luftwaffe and Naval officers for the Northern Zone.

At 0045 hours, General Toussaint, City Commandant of Prague, reports that the workforce is refusing to carry out further production of armaments and wants to start producing goods for civil use.

The order concerning the beginning of the armistice at 0800 hours German Summer Time, May 5, is sent to Commander in Chief North, Wehrmacht Commander Denmark, Naval High Command and the Luftwaffe High Command.

At 0445 hours, telexes are sent to Commander in Chief North, Wehrmacht Commander Denmark, Commander in Chief Netherlands, Naval High Command, Luftwaffe High Command and various departments of the Reich, explaining why there was an armistice in the Northern Zone while fighting continues in the east.

General Kinzl is asked to enquire whether the British wish to occupy Bornholm.

At 0730 hours, a radio message is passed to General Kinzl to be relayed to Marshal Montgomery and passed on to General Eisenhower:

"So that the tasks required by the ending of hostilities may be carried out, Grand Admiral Dönitz has appointed the officials designated below to the functions shown. Responsible for the overall direction and control of the affairs of the Reich Foreign Minister and the Reich Finance Minister: Graf Schwerin von Krosigk. Responsible for the management of the affairs of the Reich Interior Minister and the Minister of Culture: Dr. Stuckart. Responsible for the management of the affairs of the Reich Minister for Industry and Production: Speer. Responsible for the management of the affairs of the Reich Ministers of Food, Agriculture and Forestry: Backe. Responsible for the management of the affairs of the Reich Minister for Labor and Social Services: Seldte. Responsible for the management of the affairs of the Reich Minister for Transport and Postal Service: Dr. Dorpmüller."

A signal is sent to the Army Group Kurland informing them of the beginning of the armistice with Marshal Montgomery's troops.

The Commandants in the East Aegean and on Crete are informed of the conclusion of the armistice and are authorized to arrange surrender to the Anglo–Americans.

General Winter should report on the capability of the Army Group Ostmark to support the fighting withdrawal of Commander in Chief Southeast.

At 1100 hours, a message is passed to the Wehrmacht Commander Denmark, that Field Marshal Montgomery has requested General Lindemann or his chief of staff be dispatched to British General Fewing in Copenhagen before the late afternoon.

At 1424 hours, General Kinzl reports to General Jodl that parts of the Reich Air Fleet have prepared *Werwolf*.

An order explicitly forbidding this action is sent at once to Reich Air Fleet. The Grand Admiral issues orders absolutely forbidding any steps in this direction.

At 1550 hours, Commander in Chief North is informed of the conditions of the armistice which has been in force since 0800 hours, May 5, 1945. German headquarters are to carry out, immediately and without question, any orders given to them by the Allied Powers concerning any matter.

In the afternoon, Admiral Wagner and Major Friedel return from Montgomery's headquarters and report on events. Major Friedel is given documents for General Kinzl, temporary chief of the Liaison Staff with Montgomery, which are to be passed on to the Marshal.

As early as 1614 hours on May 4, the Grand Admiral had given orders to the U-boats to cease offensive operations and to return to base. He is prepared to extend the armistice to the fortresses on the Channel, the Bay of Biscay and the Channel Islands.

The text of the Instrument of Capitulation of all German armed forces in Holland, northwestern Germany (including all islands) and Denmark is sent to all German military and civilian headquarters in the Northern Zone.

Energetic action has already been taken against the Party functionary who has been broadcasting continuous calls for resistance and revolt throughout the afternoon of May 5 on the Wilhelmshaven radio.

At 1800 hours, General Kinzl reports on discussions held with Marshal Montgomery. In accordance with these discussions, a central staff is set up for the entire Northern Zone, to be headed by Field Marshal Busch. Armies, corps, divisions, etc. will be linked to equivalent British organs of command. The question of disarmament has been dealt with, as have other important matters, such as the retention of civil authorities and the protection of civilians and the wounded.

An order is sent to Naval High Command West, that it is out of the question to cross the Swiss border.

The Instrument of Capitulation is valid only with British troops. It does not apply to the Danish population or to the Danish liberation movement.

In a letter to Field Marshal Busch, Field Marshal Keitel rejects charges that a lack of dignity was evident in the ambiguous manner in which the conditions of the capitulation were made known to the civilian population.

At 1910 hours, agreement is signalled to General Löhr's proposed course of action by which he is attempting to prevent by negotiation the extermination of large sections of the Croatian people.

In the evening there is a discussion with Kinzl concerning the organization of liaison with Montgomery.

In the evening, the Grand Admiral cancels all orders concerning the scuttling of ships.

There is evident desire to ensure a smooth transition as demonstrated by the sequence of events and the manner in which they have been handled by both Germans and Allies.

May 6, 1945

In accordance with the agreement reached with the British Commander in Chief, Field Marshal Montgomery, small British occupation forces have air-landed in the Copenhagen area.

The Americans continue their advances toward the south and east in Upper Bavaria and the Alps.

The armistice is now in force in Italy following negotiations between the German and Anglo-American supreme commanders.

The disengagement movements in Croatia run according to plan. Heavy fighting continues in the Olmütz area.

The enemy is quiet on the Saxon and Silesian fronts. Seesaw battles are going on in the Frische Nehrung.

We receive reports of probing attacks from Kurland.

The Grand Admiral wishes to brief Field Marshal Kesselring personally on the new situation. At 0145 hours, Field Marshal Kesselring reports that the flight he has been ordered to make to the Grand Admiral is impossible.

He also reports that General Eisenhower has informed him that it will be pointless to send an emissary to his headquarters unless all forces commanded by Kesselring capitulate at that time to the Anglo-Americans and to the Russians. As this demand runs counter to the Grand Admiral's orders and cannot be adhered to, Kesselring has sent no plenipotentiary.

Field Marshal Kesselring's proposal to release Reich Marshal Göring from arrest is denied. On Field Marshal Keitel's orders, the present situation will be maintained.

In the morning, we receive von Friedeburg's first report on his negotiations in Eisenhower's headquarters: Eisenhower is insisting on immediate, unconditional capitulation, simultaneously on all fronts—including surrender to the Russians. The Grand Admiral orders General Jodl to fly to Eisenhower's headquarters. There, considering the situation on all fronts, he should conclude an armistice, bearing in mind the need to win maximum time for the rescue of German nationals from the eastern region.

The General flies to Rheims the same day.

In the morning, we receive reports of British advance in the Schleswig-Holstein area.

In a radio message, *Gauleiter* Uiberreither, from the Ostmark, urges the Grand Admiral to ensure that the Ostmark will be treated as part of the Reich and not as an independent entity.

After British troops occupied the airfield at Flensburg, we had no control over the German courier flights from there. Removal of restrictions is requested via the German Liaison Officer with Marshal Montgomery.

General Winter reports that food supplies in the east will last for an average of only fourteen days to three weeks. The food supply situation in the Alpine area is serious.

The garrison in the Aegean declares its loyalty.

General Löhr and all his subordinate formations are placed under the command of Commander in Chief South, Field Marshal Kesselring, effective immediately.

A signal is sent to Field Marshal Kesselring instructing him to stop independent negotiations with the Allies since General Jodl, authorized emissary for overall negotiations, is on the way to Eisenhower's headquarters. Admiral von Friedeburg, in Eisenhower's headquarters in Rheims, is also informed that General Jodl is on his way there with the Grand Admiral's authority.

1412 hours. Field Marshal Keitel informs Field Marshal Kesselring, Field Marshal Schörner and General Winter by radio that in accordance with his political task, General Eisenhower appears to be empowered to accept the general capitulation.

Despite this, he is prepared to negotiate partial capitulations with all those German forces opposing his American front and not belonging to fronts opposing the Russians.

No further resistance is to be offered to advances by American troops eastwards into the Protectorate and further to the south.

An order of battle and schematic roster of the headquarters in the Northern Zone is being prepared as a basis for the capitulation negotiations.

The food supply in Schleswig–Holstein is getting to be especially difficult due to withdrawal of our troops from Denmark.

In Denmark the British are insisting on accelerated evacuation, particularly of the cities. It has been made very clear that the troops are to capitulate to the 21st British Army Group and not to the Danes.

Repealing existing orders, the Grand Admiral now issues instructions prohibiting—effective immediately—the destruction of factories, communications facilities and consumer goods.

The following note has been received concerning the conference between General Jodl and Lieutenant General Bedell Smith on the afternoon of May 6, in Rheims:

1. Grand Admiral's objectives:
   a. to end the war as quickly as possible
   b. to preserve as many German lives as possible for the German people and to rescue them from Bolshevism.
2. The immediate capitulation creates no problems on our side:
   a. in Channel Islands and Atlantic fortresses
   b. with the remnants of the 7th Army facing the Americans
   c. in Norway.
   d. on Crete, Rhodes and Milos, as long as it takes place opposite British or American troops.
3. The situation is different concerning the capitulation in Kurland, the Vistula estuary and with the Army Groups Löhr (400,000 men), Rendulic (600,000 men), and Schörner (1,200,000 men).

   A capitulation of these armies will deliver not only the soldiers but also the German population under their protection into slavery. No German of honor can put his name to this act. The curse of millions of people would banish his name and history would brand him as a traitor. But there is also another factor. No power on earth could force the troops of the Army Groups Löhr, Rendulic and Schörner to obey an order to lay down their weapons as long as they have an open path behind them into the areas occupied by the American troops.

With the courage of desperation, they will attack anything that blocks their way and ultimately will reach you either in complete formations or in groups. But we who have signed the capitulation and have bound ourselves to observe it will be judged to have broken the treaty, and it will be declared null and void. Why then, I ask myself, are we concluding an armistice at all?

4. The conditions given to us for disarmament state explicitly:
   a. all troops are to remain in their present positions
   b. the High Command of the German Armed Forces must guarantee the execution of all orders
   c. the new government will be held responsible for continued hostilities.

There is no way out of this dilemma for us except chaos.

I am here to find a solution and ask for your help.

The conversation which followed went roughly like this:

Bedell Smith: We had played for high stakes. The war was lost once the Rhine was crossed, but we had counted on the Allies falling out. That did not happen. Concerning the difficulties for which I (Jodl) needed his help, he could not help me. As a soldier he must obey orders and must keep to the Allied agreement. He could not understand why we would not surrender to the Russians, as that would be best for us.

I answered that even if this were so, I could not now convince any German of it; as long as they saw a way open to the west they would do all in their power to take it. No order would change this. I could, however, arrange for an order to be issued that on no front should any more shots be fired at our western opponents.

I suggested the following: signing of the capitulation but not by me, rather by the commanders in chief of the three Wehrmacht services; but they could not get here before May 8 as Field Marshal Ritter von Greim would have to be located or replaced by a deputy.

We would then need not 24 but 48 hours at least, under the circumstances, to pass on these orders. With a signing on May

8, the cease fire could become effective on the afternoon of May 10.

Bedell Smith: A unilateral cessation of hostilities against the Western Allies is completely impossible. There can only be one common capitulation to all Allies. If the troops on the eastern front refused to obey clear-cut orders, then neither the German government nor the High Command of the Armed Forces could be held responsible for this. German soldiers falling back into American lines would be treated as prisoners of war.

Bedell-Smith then sought General Eisenhower's decision on this proposal. The latter rejected it out of hand and demanded: a) signing today; b) under all circumstances, the capitulation will come into force at 0000 hours, May 9; c) I would be given half an hour to consider my decision. If I refused, negotiations would be broken off and we could later negotiate with the Russians alone. The bombing raids would be resumed, and the British and American lines would be sealed off against all Germans coming from the east.

I declared that my decision could be heard from the radio signal which I would now send to Field Marshal Keitel and for whose answer I would have to wait, as I had no authority to sign.

2141 hours. Radio message from General Jodl to Field Marshal Keitel is received:

> General Eisenhower insists that we sign today; otherwise, the Allied fronts will be closed even against those attempting to surrender individually, and all negotiations will be broken off.
>
> I see no alternative—chaos or signature. Request immediate wireless confirmation as to whether I have the authority to sign the capitulation. Capitulation will then become effective. Hostilities will then cease at 0000 hours (German Summer Time), May 9, 1945. Jodl.

After midnight, a phone call is made asking Major Friedel where the answer was.

May 7, 1945

At 0130 hours, Major Friedel relays the following answer:

Grand Admiral Dönitz has given authorization to sign the capitulation under the conditions given.

signed Keitel.

At 0230 hours, General Jodl signs on behalf of the German High Command in Eisenhower's headquarters in Rheims.

Eisenhower's chief of staff, General Bedell Smith, signs for the Supreme Commander, Allied Expeditionary Forces, and General Sousloparov signs for the Russian High Command. General Sevez, deputy chief of staff of the French Army, signs as witness.

From all the Allies' orders and measures, it is clear that they are determined to use the recently gained initiative. This is especially clear in Eisenhower's insistence on immediate signature of the capitulation, rejecting any delays or suggested amendments.

In the course of the day, further details of the capitulation are made known as follows:

Under the terms of the capitulation, the undersigned General Jodl surrenders all forces unconditionally and simultaneously to the Supreme Command of the Allied Expeditionary Forces and to the Soviet High Command.

The German High Command will at once issue orders that all combat operations are to cease, effective 2300 hours Central European Time on May 8.

The surrender negotiations in Rheims are not to be considered final. They will be replaced by a general capitulation drawn up by the Allies. If the German OKW or any of the forces under their command do not concur with the terms of surrender, punitive measures will be taken.

The ratification of the final treaty of capitulation is to be carried out by the commander of the OKW and by the commanders in chief of the army, navy and air force, each vested with legal powers of attorney. The time and place will be determined by the Allies and Soviets.

At 0530 hours, General Jodl reports that negotiations on details of the execution of the capitulation will take place in General Eisenhower's headquarters at 10:00 hours on May 8. They will be concluded that morning as the General states that he will return at 1630 hours.

Other measures and decisions, aimed at rescuing as many Germans as possible from Soviet grasp and at securing food supplies, are the consequence of the laying down of arms on most fronts and the imminent effectiveness of the final general capitulation.

Appropriate orders are issued by the High Command.

At 0135 hours, Grand Admiral Dönitz issues the following order to Field Marshal Kesselring and General Winter, with copies to Army Groups Center, Ostmark and Southeast: The aim is to pull back to the West everything possible from all fronts facing the eastern enemy and—if needed—to fight your way through the Soviets. All hostilities against the Anglo-Americans are to cease at once and you are to surrender to them. General capitulation will be signed with Eisenhower today. Eisenhower has assured General Jodl that hostilities will cease effective May 9, 1945, 0000 hours German Summer Time.

Commander in Chief North, Field Marshal Busch, is responsible for maintaining discipline and order in the Holstein area. He is also responsible for the supply of food to the troops and the civilian population.

By order of the British effective immediately, the military salute will be the type used prior to the introduction of the "German salute" (otherwise known as the Hitler salute). (The Commander in Chief West has already taken this action on its own initiative.)

Army Group Kurland could not possibly avoid being captured by the Soviets as a whole, due to lack of time and naval transport capacity, and is given authority to negotiate with the local Russian commander in chief. Apart from trying to rescue as many soldiers as possible by sea, this is the only help we can given to this brave army group.

At 1245 hours, on the Flensburg radio station Reich Minister Graf Schwerin von Krosigk announces the unconditional surrender to the German people. In addition to his announcement to the U-boat crews, Grand Admiral Dönitz broadcasts messages to the Army Groups Center, South and Southeast, and to the German population of the western areas. The announcements read:

> Soldiers of the Army Groups Center, South and Southeast!
> "Together with the divisions in Kurland, in the Vistula estuary and on the Hela Peninsula, you are the last organized fighting forces, under proven leadership, still standing against the tide of Bolshevism. By doing this, you are not only protecting yourself but also millions of German men, women and children who find themselves still to the east of the American control.
>
> If you hear that in the north, west and south individual armies have laid down their weapons after an honorable fight, this has happened because the struggle against the Western Powers no longer is meaning, as the only thing we must now fight for is to rescue as many Germans as possible from Bolshevism and slavery. This is your sacred task which you must and will fulfill for the sake of our dead Führer and for the preservation of the German people in the future.
>
> Everything I currently do, politically and militarily, is done solely to save you, and the German people you protect, from destruction. However, he who thinks only of saving himself or his unit makes the rescue of the German people impossible. He is a traitor to the German people and will be treated accordingly. Unquestioned obedience, iron discipline and integrity are more essential than ever and are the absolutely indispensable prerequisite for the fulfillment of your great task. The German nation will thank you for that."

To the German populace in the occupied western areas:

> On the basis of the armistice, which has since come into effect, I call upon all German men and women to abandon any

illegal combat activity in the *Werwolf* or other organizations in those western areas occupied by the enemy, as such actions will only harm our people. All other activities and orders are superseded by the imminent general capitulation which will become effective on May 9, 0000 hours (German Summer Time), i.e. on May 8, 2300 hours according to Allied time (Central European Time).

May 8–9, 1945

In the early morning, a signal is sent to Montgomery informing him of a delay in passing the order to the U-boats at sea concerning their operational conduct in light of the terms of the capitulation.

Preparations are being made to send a liaison staff under General Fangohr to Eisenhower's headquarters.

An order is sent to Field Marshal Kesselring instructing him to direct troop movements—within the limitations of the orders given—to do everything possible to help the German population. Those Army Groups opposing the eastern enemy are given the power to enter into individual negotiations with the Soviets.

The Commandant of Bornholm receives orders to resist Soviet landing attempts.

The western fortresses are ordered to desist from destroying ships, vehicles, equipment, and ammunition.

The Grand Admiral demands close adherence to the terms of capitulation.

At 1230 hours, the Grand Admiral broadcasts the following message to the German people:

> German men and women!
> In my speech to you of May 1, in which I told the German people of the death of the Führer and my appointment as his successor, I told you that it would be my primary task to save the lives of German citizens. To achieve this aim, I gave orders to the High Command of the Armed Forces during the night of May 6–7, to declare an unconditional capitulation to all troops in all theaters of war.
> At 2300 hours, May 8, arms will fall silent.
> Soldiers of the German Wehrmacht, having proved themselves in countless battles, will now enter the bitter road into captivity and thus make the last sacrifice for the lives of women and children and for the future of our people.

We bow our heads before their demonstrated bravery and the sacrifice of the fallen and prisoners of war.

I have promised the German people that in the coming time of need, I shall do everything in my power to secure bearable living conditions for our brave women, men and children.

I do not know if I will be able to contribute much to help you in these hard times. We must look the facts in the face. The foundations on which the Reich was built have crumbled. The unity of State and Party no longer exists. The Party has abdicated its place.

With the occupation of Germany, power has passed to the occupying forces. They will decide if I and my appointed government can function. If, through exercising the powers of my office, I can be of use to my Fatherland, then I will stay in office until the will of the German people can result in the election of another head of state, or until the occupying powers render my continuance in office impossible. For it is only my love of Germany and my duty which keep me in this difficult office. Regardless of my person, I shall not stay in office one hour longer than I can with honor. That much I owe to the Reich, whose chief representative I am.

We all have a hard road before us. We must tread it with dignity, bravery and discipline as demanded by the memory of our fallen. We must tread it, harnessing all our powers of labor and achievement, because without them we will be unable to build a basis for living. We will tread it in unity and justice, without which we will not survive the coming period. We may tread it in the hope that one day our children will enjoy a free and secure existence in a peaceful Europe.

I do not wish to lag behind you on this thorny path.

If duty calls on me to stay in my office, I will try to help you in any way I can. If duty tells me to resign, then that step will also be taken in service to our people and our Reich.

At 2200 hours, the High Command of the Armed Forces broadcasts the following announcement:

On May 9, 0000 hours, the Wehrmacht services, all armed organizations or individuals in all theaters of war, shall cease hostilities directed against former opponents.

Any attempts to destroy or damage weapons, ammunition,

planes, equipment, machines of any type or to damage or sink ships run contrary to the conditions accepted and signed by the OKW and are to be prevented by all means in the overall interests of the German people.

This announcement represents an order to every man who has not yet received such an instruction through normal military channels.

Furthermore, effective May 9, 0000 hours, all Wehrmacht signal traffic is to be uncoded.

On behalf of the Grand Admiral
signed Jodl, General.

It is also ordered that all commanders are to issue written instructions to cease movements, effective May 9, 0000 hours.

To elaborate on these orders, an officer of the general staff, in the person of Colonel Meyer-Detring, has flown to Pilsen to the Army Group Schörner on the afternoon of May 7. It is especially important that this Army Group keep up the fight against the Soviets for as long as possible, as only by this means will significant German formations have the chance to use the time won to fight their way through to the Western enemies.

The most important event of this day is the summoning to Berlin of the German delegation under Field Marshal Keitel to sign the final version of the capitulation.

In addition to Keitel, this delegation includes: Admiral von Friedeburg and Luftwaffe General Stumpff and their aides-de-camp.

On May 9 at 0016 hours, the capitulation was signed for the High Command of the German Armed Forces by Field Marshal Keitel, Admiral von Friedeburg and General Stumpff, although the date on the document itself is shown as May 8. Marshal Zhukov signed for the Red Army High Command; Air Chief Marshal Tedder signed on behalf of the Supreme Commander, Allied Expeditionary Forces.

Present at the ceremony as witnesses and co-signatories were: General de Lattre de Tassigny, Commander in Chief of the First French Army; General Spaatz, Commanding General of the United States Strategic Air Forces.

ACT OF MILITARY SURRENDER

1. We the undersigned, acting by authority of the German High Command, hereby surrender unconditionally to the Supreme Commander, Allied Expeditionary Force and simultaneously to the Supreme High Command of the Red Army all forces on land, at sea, and in the air who are at this date under German control.

2. The German High Command will at once issue orders to all German military, naval and air authorities and to all forces under German control to cease active operations at 2301 hours Central European Time on 8 May 1945, to remain in the positions occupied at that time and to disarm completely, handing over their weapons and equipment to the local allied commanders or officers designated by Representatives of the Allied Supreme Commands. No ship, vessel, or aircraft is to be scuttled, or any damage done to their hull, machinery or equipment, and also to machines of all kinds, armament, apparatus, and all the technical means of prosecution of war in general.

3. The German High Command will at once issue to the appropriate commanders, and ensure the carrying out of any further orders issued by the Supreme Commander, Allied Expeditionary Force and by the Supreme High Command of the Red Army.

4. This act of military surrender is without prejudice to, and will be superseded by any general instrument of surrender imposed by, or on behalf of the United Nations and applicable to GERMANY and the German armed forces as a whole.

5. In the event of the German High Command or any of the forces under their control failing to act in accordance with this Act of Surrender, the Supreme Commander, Allied Expeditionary Force and the Supreme High Command of the Red Army will take such punitive or other action as they deem appropriate.

6. This Act is drawn up in the English, Russian and German languages. The English and Russian are the only authentic texts.

Signed at Berlin on the 8th day of May, 1945
On behalf of the German High Command
von Friedeburg   Keitel   Stumpff
IN THE PRESENCE OF:

Marshal Tedder   Marshal Zhukov
On behalf of the   On behalf of the
Supreme Commander   Supreme High Command of
Allied Expeditionary Force   the Red Army

At the signing also were present as witnesses:

de Lattre de Tassigny   General Spaatz
General Commanding in   General Commanding
   Chief   United States Strategic Air
First French Army   Forces

On May 9, the last Wehrmacht report is issued. Its contents
are as follows:

> Since midnight the weapons on all fronts have fallen silent. On
> orders by the Grand Admiral, the Wehrmacht has halted the
> fighting, which has become pointless. The heroic struggle—
> almost six years in duration—is at an end. It brought us great
> victories, but also severe defeats. In the end, the German Wehr-
> macht has succumbed to a superior foe. True to his oath, the
> German soldier has wrought immortal deeds for his people,
> which will never be forgotten.
>
> These unique efforts on the front and at home will one day be
> given their due recognition in the judgment of history. The
> efforts and sacrifices of German soldiers on land, at sea and in
> the air will be recognized even by our enemies. Every soldier
> may lay down his weapon proudly and—in this most difficult
> hour of our history—go to work bravely and confidently for the
> eternal life of our people.
>
> In this hour the Wehrmacht remembers its comrades who have
> fallen before the enemy. The fallen demand unconditional loy-
> alty, obedience and discipline to the Fatherland, which is bleed-
> ing from countless wounds.

The last fighting is taking place on the fronts opposing the Soviets.

In East Prussia, German troops are still defending themselves in the Vistula estuary and the Frische Nehrung.

The Army Group Kurland still maintains its position undefeated in the face of the superior Red Army, even after six major defensive battles.

Until the beginning of the armistice, we will continue to evacuate by air as many wounded and married men as possible.

After a defense of exemplary bravery, the defenders of the Fortress Breslau have succumbed to the enemy's superior strength.

Cease-fire orders have been transmitted to the Army Groups Center, South and Southeast.

In Bohemia and Moravia, adherence to the terms of the capitulation is being obstructed by an uprising of the Czechs.

The nightly situation conference, which is still being held daily, emphasizes that the union of the northern and southern headquarters of the Wehrmacht is urgently needed in view of the future workload.

General Jodl calls to remembrance the dead of this war and mentions the cease-fire which becomes effective at this hour.

In a radio message from Montgomery's headquarters, received at 0430 hours, the movement of German ships through the Kaiser Wilhelm Canal to western German seaports is forbidden.

A message is sent to General Eisenhower informing him that in violation of paragraph 2 of the capitulation conditions signed on May 7, artillery fire, bombings and staffings continued against the Army East Prussia's area in the Vistula estuary. Immediate stop requested.

At 1345 hours, a radio request is sent to Eisenhower requesting him to order Field Marshal Kesselring to Flensburg to report on the situation and to receive new guidelines.

The planes scheduled to pick up Fangohr's staff have not arrived, and neither has the plane scheduled to take an officer with papers for the Soviet High Command in Berlin.

Messages expressing loyalty to the commander in chief arrive from the western fortresses and the Channel Islands.

Lieutenant Colonel de Maizière, a liaison officer just returned from Kurland, reports that the spirit of the German troops there is one of faultless discipline. There are about 230,000 Germans in Kurland.

Field Marshal Kesselring informs SS *Oberstgruppenführer* [General] Sepp Dietrich that the conditions of the capitulation are also binding for Waffen-SS formations. The Field Marshal expects the Waffen-SS to conduct itself—just like the entire Wehrmacht—with complete correctness.

As the Allies have agreed to establish means of law and order, a request is made to organize a OKW Guard Battalion for the OKW.

The Allies have issued special instructions for the German Navy High Command.

May 10, 1945

The day is spent with clarification of organizational questions and issuing orders and explanations as a result of the capitulation. Connections to the Allied High Command of General Eisenhower are beginning to work.

The OKW and the government of the Reich retain a certain freedom of action in the "Enclave" agreed to by the Allies. German command sections may move freely here and are respected by the occupying powers.

In the morning, the Army High Command East Prussia reports the opening of negotiations with the Forty-Third Army of the Second Belorussian Front concerning the surrender of our formations still around Hela and in the western Vistula estuary area. Our forces there lay down their arms at 0050 hours. Arbitrary actions by Russian officers and troops are reported.

At 0430 hours, the Commander in Chief Norway reports that the British commander of the Allied forces has imposed unacceptably harsh capitulation conditions and requests cancellation. Subsequently the Commander in Chief Norway is informed of the protest actions taken and reminded that it is necessary to protest against unjust terms on the spot.

The Wehrmacht commander in Denmark also reports encroachments by the British and lodges protest. The OKW fully supports this protest and sends a radio message to General Fangohr, commander of the German Liaison Staff who is to be flown to General Eisenhower's headquarters in Rheims, giving full details of both the Danish and Norwegian situations so that a protest may be lodged with Allied headquarters.

General Winter, Southern Zone, is informed that the Wehrmacht will handle all questions concerning commerce and food supply for the civilian population until further notice.

The Reich ministries nominate deputies for the Northern and Southern Zones. The OKW is working together with Field

Marshal Busch in the Northern Zone and Field Marshal Kesselring in the Southern Zone in accordance with Eisenhower's instructions.

The supplementary conditions of the capitulation signed in Berlin are transmitted to all army commands and to all headquarters reporting to the OKW. They are:

"All German military, naval and air authorities and all forces under German control are to disarm completely, handing over their weapons and equipment to the local allied commanders or officers designated by Representatives of the Allied Supreme Commands."

General Eisenhower is informed by radio that the Army Groups Center and South have confirmed receipt of the OKW's order with the supplementary capitulation conditions. It is known that Field Marshal Schörner has issued strict orders to adhere to the terms of the capitulation to the letter. It is not known whether part of the troops have disobeyed this order or if the Czech liberation movement has made it difficult for them to obey the order, as there is no radio contact with the Army Groups Center, South or Southeast at the moment.

At 1630 hours, a radio message is sent to the commander in Bornholm instructing him to regard Bornholm as part of Denmark:

"A clear capitulation treaty has been concluded with Field Marshal Montgomery concerning German troops in Denmark. Any capitulation concluded under pressure from the Russians is to be considered invalid.

"All further steps to be cancelled; await Allied Supreme Headquarter's decision, which has been requested."

At 1842 hours, there is a radio message from General Eisenhower:

"Field Marshal Kesselring's flight to OKW is not approved. On May 11, General Eisenhower wishes the following persons to be sent to his headquarters:

1. Secretary of State of the Reich government.
2. Senior signal traffic officer of the Luftwaffe.
3. Most senior OKW intelligence officer.

The discussion will last for some days."

At 2350 hours, General Eisenhower is asked by radio when planes will be made available for the liaison commission staff requested by Marshal Zhukov's chief of staff. Fangohr's delegation for Rheims is also ready to travel. Notification of estimated time of take-off from Flensburg is requested.

From the above it is clear that the organization of mutual communications is still very inadequate.

In place of the non-authorized flight of Marshal Kesselring to the OKW, a flight for the Deputy Chief of Wehrmacht Operations Staff General Winter to the OKW is requested but again refused by Eisenhower. The complete dependence on the wishes of the Allies is emphasized by refusals of this type.

Due to changes in the overall situation, a reorganization of the OKW has become necessary and an order to this effect is issued.

May 11, 1945

The course of events demonstrates again how varied daily events are even after the capitulation.

The commandants of St. Nazaire and Lorient are the last fortress commandants to close down transmission. With this action, all the western fortresses and the Channel Islands have confirmed compliance with the terms of the capitulation and have ceased communicating with us.

From the point of their disembarking in the area of the Commander in Chief North, all troops arriving from Rügen, East and West Prussia and Kurland are under his command.

Army High Command East Prussia requests that the Second Belorussian Front ensure that radio communications between the OKW and Army High Command East Prussia continue to be guaranteed even beyond May 12, 1945.

Allied headquarters have decided that the island of Bornholm, along with its garrison, should initially be surrendered to the Soviets. Future disposition will be decided later.

The Reich Air Fleet will receive its orders concerning demobilization directly from the 2nd Tactical Air Force.

The Navy is informed that decisions on basic rules concerning flags and emblems of state have been requested from Supreme Allied Headquarters.

The expression "capitulation" is to replace the word "cease-fire."

The area of the OKW has been designated a special zone.

In questions of demobilization, the Reich Labor Service is to be treated similar to the Wehrmacht.

At 1610 hours, a telex is sent to Fangohr's Liaison Staff in Rheims requesting permission for broadcasts to be made from the Flensburg Radio and two other mobile broadcast transmitters.

In various radio messages, General Winter reports that he has received definition of the tasks of Kesselring's staff. He requests a territorial separation of the Northern and Southern Zones. At 1634 hours, he reports that the staff of General Löhr, Commander in Chief Southeast, has apparently been captured by Tito.

He further requests that the accumulated supplies of bread and grain still held in the Bohemia–Moravia area be released for distribution.

An order of the Grand Admiral concerning relations with the occupying powers—and especially that of German servicemen—is distributed to the troops. It says:

> We must allow our former opponents to approach us, and we must meet them with decency and politeness.
>
> We stand with unblemished honor as soldiers and may justly stand up full of pride and dignity.
>
> Every soldier will stay at his post until he receives further orders from his superior. The timing of demobilization depends upon the decisions of the occupying powers and the transport facilities.

May 12, 1945

In Norway the local Wehrmacht Commander, General Böhme, has protested to Supreme Allied Headquarters that both headquarters and troops regard it as an insult that they are ordered to disarm and intern their own German soldiers (SS). As far as discipline and attitude toward their superiors are concerned, there is no difference between the members of an organization subject to an insulting special ruling and the main body of the troops. To avoid further blows to the troops' morale and possible irreparable damage to their discipline, General Böhme formally requests to be allowed to refrain from carrying out the Allied capitulation conditions for his troops, namely to arrest a particular group of persons.

Details of the regulation of official communications with Allied headquarters are formalized. A list is issued concerning questions of cooperation between Germans and the Allies.

Since the Reich government and the OKW are located in a so-called special area, the internal executive power is established in a meeting with Brigadier Churcher, British commandant of Flensburg, who is the local representative of Allied executive power.

A renewed request is made by the OKW via the liaison staff of General Kinzl at Field Marshal Montgomery's 21st British Army Group, that it approve establishment of a motorized OKW Guard Battalion as a pro-forma police force. Difficulties become apparent.

Field Marshal Busch reports, for example, that he cannot take responsibility for the tasks assigned to him by Field Marshal Montgomery in the assigned area since he has neither weapons nor appropriate influence.

At 1215 hours, a radio message is received from that part of the OKW located with Field Marshal Kesselring's staff in the Southern Zone and commanded by the Deputy Chief of OKW Operations Staff General Winter. According to this report, the whereabouts of the Army Group Ostmark (formerly South) and the Commander in Chief Southeast are unclear, due to the confusing developments in the Balkans.

The following official position is declared, concerning the legal status and content of the unconditional capitulation declared on May 8, 1945:

"Our Western opponents have always maintained during the war—and this has been explicitly confirmed in the statements made on the occasion of the capitulation—that their aim has been to restore the rule of law in international relationships. Our opponents will therefore not wish to expose themselves before world opinion to charges of using methods similar to those against which they went to war, particularly now that the Führer—who according to them is the mainspring of tyranny—is dead."

In the daily situation conference, General Jodl gives guidance for our communications with the Allies, suggesting that the Allied delegations be bombarded with proposals and memos.

He says, "They must be confronted with the great organizational questions that must be solved as a result of the total collapse. It must also be made clear to them that we Germans love life but do not fear death. In all discussions with the Allies, Grand Admiral Dönitz is to be referred to as Supreme Commander of the Wehrmacht and not as head of state."

May 13, 1945

It is now possible to form a general overview of the progress of the capitulation. The following picture emerges:

Norway: The marching movements are proceeding according to plan. German troops are quartered in reservations (120 of the smallest villages). The arrival of an Allied formation in Oslo by sea has been announced for May 13. Until now, one division equivalent of Allied troops has arrived in Norway.

Denmark: Movements proceeding according to plan. Following British orders, German troops are being concentrated in the Eiderstedter peninsula; 33,700 men have arrived there so far.

In the district of Schleswig, the British have employed the Brigade *Grossdeutschland* as a security force.

A protest by General Lindemann against measures taken by the British Major General Fewing evokes a response from Fewing. He makes certain allowances to German troops regarding the retention of bicycles, ambulances and personal possessions as well as motorized and horse-drawn vehicles.

Netherlands: Things are proceeding according to plan. According to instructions from the First Canadian Army, the exchange of signals between General Blaskowitz and Lieutenant General Straube must stop.

Southern Zone: The formations under command of Commander in Chief West have met American demands. They are being assembled in collection camps. The Americans have approved organizing security forces of German military police and 100 men per division.

Trieste has been occupied by Yugoslavia. The final ownership of Trieste will be decided at the peace negotiations.

Soviet Russia: The OKW still has no communications with Marshal Zhuhov's staff. We also know nothing of the fate of Lieutenant Colonel of the General Staff de Maizière who was ordered to Berlin by plane to act as liaison officer. The

Russians simply refuse to answer queries directed to them by the American headquarters.

Kurland: Evacuation by sea of a small part of the troops has been carried out with excellent discipline, according to reports by both the army and navy. Available shipping space has been fully exploited. For example, on S-boats with a 23-man crew, another 220 men have been taken on board; mine-sweepers with a crew of 60 have transported about 700 men. After disembarking, these undefeated troops marched to their barracks, some in parade step.

Channel Islands: The transfer to the British is proceeding in a dignified manner.

With the exception of the Kurland front, we have no news of developments from the eastern front and of the fate of millions of Germans. They are in the hands of the Soviets and are, therefore, cut off from the rest of the world.

In a special enclave of the supreme Reich authorities, a ministerial conference takes place at 1000 hours at Foreign Minister Graf Schwerin von Krosigk's office. He announces the main topics of news from the British and American press. According to this, no German newspapers are to be published for the time being.

The Allies regard the question of feeding the population as very critical. Based on a discussion with British experts, Minister Backe believes that the British are well-informed of German food supply problems. According to British announcements, the organization of German food production is to be retained largely intact. British troops are to be supplied with food from their own logistical system and will not draw on the German market.

In the course of the day, an Allied Control Commission begins to operate under the direction of American Major General Rooks in Flensburg.

General Rooks, as well as the other members of the Allied Control Commission, live on the modern motor ship *Patria* of the Hamburg–Süd Line, lying in Flensburg harbor.

At 1055 hours, General Rooks requests by phone that the

Grand Admiral visit him on the *Patria* at 1200 hours, and Field Marshal Keitel at 1230 hours.

At 1200 hours Grand Admiral Dönitz and General Rooks meet on the *Patria.*

General Rooks presents himself as plenipotentiary of the Allied Supreme Commander, General Eisenhower, and states that he is instructed to work with the Grand Admiral. He discloses that Allied Headquarters has directed that Field Marshal Keitel is to be relieved of his position as Chief of the OKW, and is to consider himself a prisoner of war, effective immediately. As temporary replacement for Field Marshal Keitel, General Eisenhower has chosen General Jodl. Rooks adds that he looks forward to fruitful cooperation with the OKW. He considers himself as a representative of the military government agencies.

Grand Admiral Dönitz replies that as head of state he is also the Supreme Commander of the Wehrmacht and uses the OKW to carry out his orders. The Grand Admiral states further that the most critical problems at the moment are to find solutions for the food supply, currency circulation and the revival of the transport system.

General Rooks shares the Grand Admiral's views and confirms that Allied Supreme Command is eager to find solutions to these urgent questions. The Grand Admiral suggests the formation of one central agency which can manage jointly all problems. General Rooks agrees and predicts an appropriate solution will be found. General Rooks acknowledges the correctness of the Grand Admiral's position and the measures which he has taken so far.

At 1230 hours a meeting takes place between General Rooks and Field Marshal Keitel on board the *Patria.* General Rooks informs the Field Marshal that on General Eisenhower's orders he has been removed from his position as Chief of the OKW, effective immediately, and is to consider himself a prisoner of war. He has the task of picking up the Field Marshal at 1430 hours to take him to the airfield for further transportation. The Field Marshal may choose to take along an aide-de-camp, an orderly and bring along a reasonable amount of luggage. General Jodl has been appointed his temporary successor.

Field Marshal Keitel makes no response to this announcement except to say that he himself signed the unconditional surrender and understands the consequences of that action.

At 1430 hours, a discussion takes place on the *Patria* between the Commander of the Control Commission at the OKW, General Rooks and General Jodl.

General Rooks states that he has the task of monitoring orders issued by the OKW. He announces the removal of Field Marshal Keitel from his post, his arrest, and the temporary appointment of General Jodl to act as deputy in Keitel's place as Chief of the OKW. General Rooks requests free access for himself and his officers to all offices of the OKW. He further requests agreement on the operating procedures with himself and his staff. General Rooks expects only to have to deal with basic questions concerning the three branches of the Wehrmacht.

General Jodl replies that he will carry out orders in accordance with the compliance with the conditions of the capitulation to the best of his knowledge and conscience. The General states, "I will always come to you to request the cessation of any measures which are liable to further increase the misfortune of the German people. I will always come if the honor of German soldiers and of the German people is being trampled in the dust by the actions of local commanders. I repeat again that I consider it my sole duty to help the German people by carrying out your orders to the best of my ability, and conscience."

General Jodl further requests clarification of important organizational questions for the purpose of successful operation and states that he will present proposals to this effect. General Rooks will be expecting these proposals. During this meeting, other matters are discussed, particularly that of war decorations and national emblems worn on German uniforms which currently all bear the swastika. This question is now awaiting a decision at Allied headquarters.

Finally, the General explains to General Rooks that since

April 24, 1945 there has been no division between the High Command of the Armed Forces and the Army High Command.

By order of the Grand Admiral, General Jodl assumes duties as Chief of the OKW, in addition to his existing responsibilities. General Jodl intends to present the following proposal to General Rooks after their discussion:

1. Division of Germany into three areas:
   a. 21st British Army Group cooperation with Field Marshal Busch, Commander in Chief North.
   b. 12th American Army Group cooperation with General Obstfelder, Seventh Army.
   c. 6th American Army Group cooperation with Lieutenant General Schultz, Army Group G.
2. Request to combine elements of the OKW from the Northern and Southern Zones.
3. Further proposals will be prepared concerning desirable organizational structure within the areas of the Reich.

During the situation conference, General Jodl states that the demarcation between the Russian and American spheres of interest is not yet known.

With reference to the food supply problem, he states that Reich Minister Backe is convinced, based on discussions with the British that they are aware of the seriousness of our situation.

Jodl further states that we will need a reference map showing all German borders as well as those of Czechoslovakia and Austria as they were on September 1, 1939, to be able to refer to it in discussions with the Allies.

Jodl: "We will have to approach the Allies as dictated by our difficult position. We have capitulated unconditionally because we carried the war into the final phase and consequences. There are to be no reminiscences of 1918. We cannot help ourselves; we must rely on the help of others. This means that the major thrust of all our actions must be in the political sector. The role of Germany as a nation in the center of Europe is not yet over. Without Germany there can be no long-term solution to the problems.

"We must protest against all Allied actions which affect our honor. The Allied Commission must recognize German problems; therefore we must submit proposals to them. All matters of substance arising from discussions with the Allies must be brought to the attention of interested departments."

Field Marshal Keitel has been flown out as a prisoner of war. The General is filled with deep sympathy.

The reason for his arrest is probably that Field Marshal Keitel, in his position as Chief of the OKW, had to pass on an order of the Führer's directing the liquidation of 50 English officers who broke out of a prisoner of war camp in April 1944. This, at least, is the General's personal opinion.

The General announces that he has temporarily taken over the duties of the Chief of the OKW on the orders of the Grand Admiral and with Eisenhower's approval. He expects that everyone, particularly the officers, will conduct themselves as loyal and respectable soldiers in this situation.

Concerning his new task, General Jodl says the following: "I feel called to master even the greatest task." He adds, "For five years I have kept silent and obeyed, asking nothing for myself, merely working. I am an obedient soldier and have looked upon it as an honor to maintain this obedience in accordance with my oath. In these five years I have worked and remained silent even though I sometimes had completely different opinions.

"I wish to reintroduce the traditional virtues, in particular those of the work of the German general staff, as they once were practiced. I shall act only in accordance with the old, tested principles."

1. April 29, 1945 — British "Buffalo" armored amphibians cross the Elbe to reinforce the British bridgehead near Lüneberg.

2. British troops meet the Russians on May 3, 1945 in Mecklenburg.

3. Field Marshal Montgomery with the German delegation at the signing of the capitulation in the Northern Zone on May 4, 1945. From left to right: Field Marshal Montgomery, Admiral von Friedeburg, General Kinzel, Rear Admiral Wagner, Major of the General Staff Friedel.

4. Admiral von Friedeburg signs the capitulation of the German forces in the Northern Zone in the presence of Field Marshal Montgomery on May 4, 1945 in Lüneburg.

5. The overall capitulation of the German Wehrmacht in General Eisenhower's headquarters in Rheims on May 7, 1945. From left to right: Major of the General Staff Oxenius, General Jodl, Admiral von Friedeburg.

6. General Eisenhower after the German capitulation in Rheims on May 7, 1945.

7. Refugees from the Eastern Provinces are lifted to safety in the *Seedienst Ostpreussen*.

8. A group of parliamentarians in front of the combat headquarters of a German combat group in Prague in the morning of May 8, 1945, on the way from Pilsen to Wolkow near Jaromir to meet the Army Group Schörner. From the right, front row: Colonel of the General Staff Meyer-Detring, OKW Operations Staff; Lieutenant Colonel Pratt, G3 V (Operations Officer) U.S. Corps, with interpreter. Back row: commander of a German combat group, Czech Gendarmerie officer as guide, two American officers of the convoy, a German combat group officer.

9. Arrival in Berlin on May 8, 1945 of the German delegation for the signing of the "unconditional surrender." From left to right: General Skumpf, Field Marshal Keitel, Admiral von Friedeburg.

10. A Russian photograph of the "unconditional surrender" ceremony in Berlin-Karlshorst. Field Marshal Keitel in the act of signing; in the center, U.S. General Spaatz; to his right, Marshal Zhukov.

11. Field Marshal Keitel signs the German capitulation on May 8, 1945 in the Soviet headquarters in Berlin-Karlshorst.

12. As part of the Allies' victory parade over Hitler Germany in May 1945 in Berlin, General Zhukov and Field Marshal Montgomery are seen in front of the Brandenburg Gate.

13. On the occasion of the internment of Dönitz's government in Flensburg-Mürwik, male and female staff members are guarded by soldiers with fixed bayonets, under degrading conditions.

14. 10.00 hours, May 23, 1945: internment of Dönitz's government. Civilian and military staff members are led away.

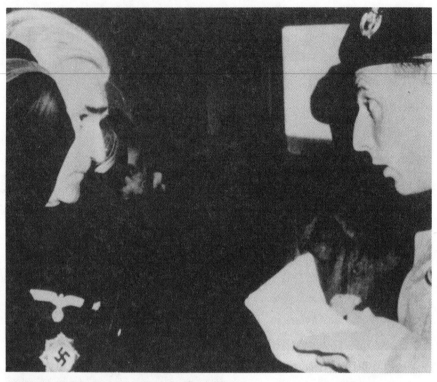

15. Internment of Dönitz's government. Interrogation of Rear Admiral Wagner, who is forced to hold his hands behind his head as he answers questions from a British interrogation officer.

16. Internment of Grand Admiral Dönitz on May 23, 1945 by the British in Flensburg-Mürwik.

17. The Battle for Berlin. Old and young soldiers with bazookas.

18. The commander of a burning Soviet tank, who managed to get out of the wreck, excitedly shouts encouragement to his comrades to continue the fight.

19. Russian infantry advances through the burning Tiergarten area toward the Reich Chancellery.

20. The end in Berlin, May 1945, after the street fighting.

21. Wrecked German scout car in the courtyard of the embattled Reich Chancellery.

22. The entrance to the Führer's bunker in the Reich Chancellery.

23. Bullet holes, traces of shell splinters, and Cyrillic writing mark the bronze plate of the Reich Chancellery after the capture of Berlin.

24. The end of the Battle for Berlin.

25. General Weidling, Combat Commandant of Berlin.

26. General Busse, Commander in Chief of the Ninth Army committed to relieve Berlin.

27. General Wenck, Commander in Chief of the Twelfth Army sent to relieve Berlin.

28. Waffen-SS General Steiner, Commander of the Steiner Group committed to relieve Berlin.

29. General Gotthard Heinrici, Commander in Chief of the Army Group Vistula.

30. General Krebs as an emissary outside General Chuikov's headquarters.

31. Marshal Georgi Zhukov, Commander in Chief of the First Belorussian Front and Konev's rival.

32. Marshal Vassili J. Chuikov. At the time of the capture of Berlin, he commanded the 8th Guards Army as a general.

33. Marshal Ivan S. Konev (left), Commander in Chief of the First Ukranian Front, in 1945.

34. General Weidling, Combat Commandant of Berlin, capitulated on May 2, 1945. In this original Russian photograph, he is seen leaving the bunker of the Reich Chancellery on May 6. The Russians had Weidling identify Goebbel's body. This bunker was never a command post; however, the Russians wrote on this photo, "General Weidling, leaving his command bunker," and used it as propaganda for the film "Capitulation of Berlin."

35. The ruins of Berlin in May 1945.

May 14, 1945

The day brings a further intensification of cooperation with the Allies. Numerous organizational measures are decreed.

A report comes in from Norway that the expected British naval force reached Oslo on May 13.

The British have organized prisoner of war areas on the Eiderstedter peninsula for the troops from Denmark, on the Oldenburger peninsula (Oldenburg in Holstein) for troops from the east, and near Cuxhaven/Stade for troops between the Weser and Elbe.

Radio communications have been reestablished with East Prussia. The evacuation of Hela progresses rapidly.

We may assume that almost all wounded have been evacuated from the area of the Vistula and from Hela.

The surrender of the Army East Prussia to the Russians with 150,000 men was completed on May 14, at 1200 hours.

Moscow reports the capture of 180,000 men in Kurland. No special reports are received from the Southern Zone.

Navy: So far 14 U-boats have entered Allied harbors. About 40 U-boats are still underway. Five German and two Italian U-boats are in Japan.

Luftwaffe: The Allied Commission reaches a decision concerning the command relationships of the Luftwaffe—they are to remain unchanged.

Cooperation with the Allies: A proposal concerning cooperation between German and Allied headquarters is submitted as follows:

OKW, with General Eisenhower;

Commander in Chief North, with 21st British Army Group;

Army High Command Norway, with the Allied commander in Norway;

Commander in Chief West, with 12th American Army Group;

Army Group G, Lieutenant General Schultz, with 6th American Army Group;

Commander in Chief Southeast, von Vietinghoff, with the 14th Allied Army Group.

A proposal for the Luftwaffe is being prepared.

The Chief Signals Officer submits a proposal for the Signal Corps. The aim is to demonstrate how vital the choice of a central location is to secure communications.

In the civil sector, the Chief of Staff of the Allied Commission has ordered State Secretaries Rieke and Reich to appear the Allied Commission to discuss questions of rationing and supply. Efforts to deal with these difficulties can be seen taking shape with the British and Americans; the British especially have realized that they must take action.

The resolution of specialist problems is causing difficulties both with the government and with the OKW because the bulk of the government members, including the specialists, are still in southern Germany.

The Chief of the Control Commission at the OKW is requested to release broadcast transmitters. The Control Commission replies that the request has been forwarded to headquarters for action.

The Control Commission is informed that the files and data concerning food, clothing and other supplies requested at short notice for the area of Commander in Chief North cannot supplied, due to lack of signal communication facilities.

The Control Commission is given data concerning the transport facilities available. This data is incomplete as neither the Wehrmacht Chief Transport Officer nor the Reich Ministries are allowed freedom of movement. In addition, the State Railway communications network is not yet working.

General Jodl issues an order concerning working relationships with the occupying powers.

In the daily situation conference Jodl emphasizes that, in his view, the Allies are placing special value on counter-intelligence documents but that none were available.

Jodl elaborates: "We can only continue to repeat that, by Hitler's orders, the Wehrmacht was excluded from major questions of intelligence. Hitler delegated the conduct of intelligence operations to the *Reichssicherheitshauptamt* (Central Office of State Security) because he did not trust the Wehrmacht to carry out this task to his satisfaction. In his opinion, this relieves the Wehrmacht of a great deal of responsibility provides the Wehrmacht with a case of extenuating circumstances. Furthermore, there will be found much extenuating material in favor of the Wehrmacht among many documents.''

In closing, Jodl reviews future political opportunities, which could be caused by the serious differences between East and West. In this view, the General is probably influenced by reports from the chief of the attaché department who had conversations with the Russians in Berlin on May 8–9, 1945 during the signing of the capitulation. He had formed the opinion that there were also political chances with the Russians.

May 15, 1945

The disestablishment necessitated by the signing of the capitulation proceed further on May 15.

No special reports are received from Norway or the Northern Zone.

Communist propaganda has been found in the holding camp in Hamburg. Leaflets have been posted. Due to uncertainty about future developments, the morale in some of the prisoner of war camps is low.

0830 hours, we finally have telephone connection with Eisenhower's staff in Rheims.

Reich Minister Backe has been summoned to Eisenhower for negotiations.

On May 14 Field Marshal Kesselring was flown to General Eisenhower's headquarters on his orders. It is not known if he will return. The senior commander in chief in the Southern Zone is now General Dessloch.

Since the Americans have repealed the Flag Law of 1935, it is unclear which flag is currently valid.

The Occupying Powers take over the State Railway. The commander of the Allied Control Commission with the OKW places a limitation on the orders transmitted by the OKW to subordinate headquarters. In answer to a renewed request to release broadcast transmitters, the Control Commission replies that the matter is being considered but that no final decision has yet been made. The Allied Control Commission prohibits soldiers from singing on the roads. They may only whistle. Since the morning of May 13, Army Lindemann (Denmark) has been reporting that the British routinely confiscated trucks and cars.

A protest is made since it violates the terms of the capitulation.

From the southeast comes news of the pursuit and disarmament of a German combat group by Yugoslavian forces. In

Czechoslovakia German troops continue to try to avoid capture by the Soviets and to give themselves up to the Americans. Since the day of the capitulation, there has been heavy fighting here between German troops and Czechoslovakian rebels. The Red Army has also broken into the Bohemia-Moravia area. On May 9 Prague was captured by Marshal Konev's tanks.

Schörner's Army Group, split up into combat groups, is still fighting to avoid capture by the Bolsheviks and Czechs. It is a desperate last struggle.

In Austria the independence of the Austrian Republic is proclaimed.

From the Southern Zone, General Winter requests that we ask the Soviets to release for distribution the grain trains in Bohemia which are earmarked to feed the civilian population.

He further requests that the staff of Commander in Chief West be removed from the chain of command following Kesslering's removal to Eisenhower and that the detached OKW South be placed under his direct command.

The Navy reports that additional submarines have put into Allied harbors. Thirteen U-boats are reported as still being at sea; in addition, twenty-six boats are still at sea but have not reported in.

To avoid incidents, Grand Admiral Dönitz orders that pictures of leading personalities of the Third Reich be removed from offices where members of the Allied Control Commission may be expected to visit.

The question of the requirement to salute and of medals and orders is also being considered.

In the afternoon, the offices of the OKW and the Navy are inspected by the commander of the British Control Commission, Brigadier (General) Foord.

During the situation conference under direction of General Jodl, the following remarkable closing sentence from the May 12 Daily Report of the Information Department of the Reich government is announced. It says:

> Amidst all this it is clear that Germany, even in its state of total defeat, has become a factor in Europe. The Grand Admir-

al's government and the Allies' acceptance of it—in however limited a form—is external proof of this.

Perhaps the deeper meaning of its existence lies in the fact, that in these days of dissolution it is representing the Reich's sovereignty and thus preserves this unity through the capitulation and into a new era.

General Jodl adds the following comment from the viewpoint of the highest authorities of the Reich:

All protests and complains must be based upon international law. Unfortunately, we have never used the weapon of justice in recent times. We have broken laws—to be sure, only after the enemy has set the example—but we have not worked within the limits of justice by which we could have achieved far more than we did by using force.

The attitude towards the enemy powers must be: You fought the war for justice, thus we demand to be treated under the law.

We must continually refer the Allies to international law. Law is the basis of every human community. The laws of states and peoples must supersede that of every individual. Regarding our compliance with the capitulation agreement, we must emphasize to the Allies where the borderline is, namely then, when our honor is impugned.

This point is to be referred to repeatedly in open conversation. If an Allied measure affects our honor, e.g. removal and banning of war decorations or similar steps, then incalculable consequences may occur, e.g. the surrender of weapons will be jeopardized, etc.

But apart from this, we want to move the Control Commission to the conviction that we are dealing correctly. In this way we will gradually win their confidence. Then, when the groundwork has been laid by our loyal attitude, the Grand Admiral will meet with Eisenhower, and discuss with him issues concerning the future.

The General is convinced that at this time the Allies have no plans to install an emigré government.

The General issues a warning to the advocates of the solution that the Wehrmacht should become the executive power;

he is not convinced that this solution—the Wehrmacht running the government—is one he can support, because the enemy would then conclude that the OKW would suffice to run the government. In this case, the Wehrmacht would then be responsible for feeding the German people, a task which the Wehrmacht can in no way carry out. In addition, the Wehrmacht is only capable of managing certain areas of government, e.g. communications and transport.

The occupying powers have de facto recognized Grand Admiral Dönitz as head of state, because the power of attorney for those who signed the capitulation, as demanded by the Allies, bore his signature and was approved by the other side.

The first act in the reconstruction of Germany is the most loyal execution of all tasks the Allies impose.

As to the question of classified information, we have nothing to hide. We planned operations and carried them out. We maintained loyalty and obedience and, even now, we regard as a traitor anyone who has not been obedient. When dealing with the Allies, the word "protest" should be avoided; one should use alternative means of expression, such as pointing out consequences, by saying that this and that would happen which could not be in the Allied interest.

The Grand Admiral intends to issue an order in which he will distance himself sharply from the issue of the excesses in the treatment of concentration camp inmates.

Churchill's recent speech contains a reference to Hitler's fatal mistake, that of attacking Russia.

Jodl: "I am convinced that if we had not declared war on Russia, we would have won. We did not attack Russia because we wanted the space but because—day by day—the Russian concentration of forces increased tremendously and would finally have led to an ultimatum.

"It is the view of some people that this question could have been solved politically, either by 'talking to' the Russians (they would have denied their war preparations and referred to the treaty between us), or by asking the British to intervene, and they would have ridiculed us and said, 'That would be the best

thing that could happen for us, if Russia also declared war on
you.' "

It is known that the attempt to reach an agreement with
Molotov during his last visit to Germany had failed.

According to Jodl's statement, Hitler declared war on Russia
not on the basis of prior political aims, but rather in response
to pressing necessities.

Jodl: "All of us—and especially every soldier—entered this
war against Russia with a feeling of foreboding when considering its outcome. It was made particularly clear to me in the
catastrophe of the winter of 1941–42, that from this culminat-
ing point at the beginning of 1942 victory could no longer be
won. The high point had been passed and even the renewed,
initially successful, attempt to change our fortunes in the
summer of 1942, failed."

May 16, 1945

Additional British naval formations have arrived in Norway. The troop movements in Army High Command Norway and Army Lindemann are running according to plan.

In the Commander in Chief North's sector the behavior of the British is generally correct.

In addition to the collecting camps on the Eiderstedter and Oldenburger peninsulas and in the Cuxhaven–Stade areas, others are being set up on the North Sea islands of Pellworm and Nordstrand and in Dithmarschen. These collecting camps are for all practical purposes prisoner of war camps.

The Second British Army will not permit dispersion of troops and refugees south across the Elbe, on the grounds that the northwestern German area should remain reserved for the civilian population to be evacuated from the devastated areas of the Ruhr, and perhaps also for the 20th Army, Army High Command Norway.

According to reports from Commander in Chief North, the British seem to want to allow local commanders to deal with most issues. Objections by Army Groups and Armies are thus largely limited.

In the Southern Zone, 31,390 agricultural workers from the *Volkssturm* have been released. It seems that the Allies have turned 20,000 German prisoners of war over to the Italians for reconstruction work.

We have the following report from the Navy: several British minesweepers have arrived in the Elbe estuary. The North Sea islands have been or are being occupied. Sea transports of troops and refugees are debarking in Kiel, Neustadt in Holstein and Wilhelmshaven.

Twenty U-boats have arrived in Allied harbors. Thirteen U-boats have reported in as being at sea; in addition, there are 41 boats at sea. This figure, however, is questionable. Probably there are 11 boats at sea which have not yet reported, and 94 boats in foreign ports. A listing for German harbors follows.

General Fangohr, commander of the liaison staff with General Eisenhower, reports that the Danish island of Bornholm, up until now under German occupation, has been handed over to the Russians.

During a meeting with General Newins, Chief of Operations in General Eisenhower's headquarters, Fangohr was told, "Your status and that of your liaison staff is now that of prisoners of war."

Lieutenant Colonel de Maizière has returned. He reports on his visit to Marshal Zhukov's Soviet headquarters. He was absolutely, correctly treated. The questions asked of him all related to explanations of the documents that he had carried with him. All questions Lieutenant Colonel de Maizière submitted remained unanswered. Lieutenant Colonel de Maizière was questioned in great detail about the organization of the Army General Staff and the Wehrmacht Operations Staff.

General Westphal, Chief of Staff Commander in Chief West, reports that the exclusion from the chain of command of Commander in Chief West staff, as proposed by General Winter, would adversely affect the supply operations for the troops, particularly during these hard times.

An order is issued directing the troops to salute officers of the occupying power.

In a meeting of ministers on May 16, it is noted that the Reich currently has no legally authorized flag. An interim solution must be urgently sought.

The issues most urgently requiring solutions are: food supply, transportation and finance.

Reich Minister Backe is expected to return from Eisenhower's headquarters on May 17.

The Allied Control Commission wishes to speed up bringing together representatives of the Ministry of Transport for the purpose of restoring communications. Dorpmüller and Ganzenmüller have been chosen.

During the situation conference, General Jodl supports the thoughts of the Reich Foreign Minister concerning the language to be used when discussions with the Allies turn to National Socialism etc. The official position will be: "After the First World War, we suffered hunger and privation. The result was a turn toward National Socialism. If you Allies wish to bring about even worse hunger after this war by your actions, there will be a reaction. As a result, those Germans who still have any spirit will turn to communism."

If the question of the concentration camps is raised and we Germans are condemned because of it, I ask, 'Why don't you Allies get worked up about Russia?'

"Never comment on matters not within the area of your competence. You must look at everyone present before answering. Otherwise it can easily happen that a smart reporter is present who will turn a harmless remark around and distort it into the opposite.

"According to Churchill's statement, the present government is to be regarded as an administration.

"We must avoid getting into conflict with the military Control Commission. We must always bear in mind that our opposition will be waiting for an opportunity to mistreat and humiliate us.

"We are just at the beginning of a painful period which will last for months and years. That which awaits us in our future will be more depressing than ever.

"For reasons as yet unknown to us, the British are currently somewhat loosening the reins."

May 17–22, 1945

In these days the execution of the terms of the capitulation is proceeding more or less quickly. The consequences of the total defeat become clearer day by day.

The daily situation reviews nevertheless continue to be held until May 20, 1945. At these conferences, General Jodl repeatedly voices his opinion on the most important military and political questions of the day and on internal matters raised as a result of our contact with the Allies.

Although the present government is to be regarded as an adminstration, according to Churchill's statements, this qualification, made by an authoritative source, is at least a recognition of a German governmental institution.

On May 18, Jodl announces that in the next few days the area currently occupied by the Americans east of the Elbe–Trave Canal, i.e. western Mecklenburg and western Mark Brandenburg, is to be handed over to the Russians. The question of the status of Lübeck is still unclear.

At one conference Jodl says, "There is still no clarity as to the Russians' position. It is quite possible that the Russians will soon have their occupied zone better organized and administered than the Western Powers in their occupation zones.

"The Russians will try—and have already started to do so through propaganda—to attract as many Germans as possible into their zone, or at least to make the prospect attractive. If we take the path to the east and go over to the Russians, this can and probably will lead to the death of our people. After the extermination of the intelligentsia, German nationals would be absorbed by Slavic civilization.

"One must always allude to this possibility. There is no doubt that we cannot talk of the war as being ended until the three great powers—America, Great Britain and Russia—have reached agreement.

"The question is: do the Russians want this agreement? At

the moment they possess a great land army in comparison to the Allies. In addition, they have all the materiel they captured from us. To oppose them, the Western Allies have only their superior air forces.

"To all those who ask what will happen, we can only say 'Wait and see!' But one thing is sure, if the British and Americans maintain their present behavior, it will result in disaster."

Jodl stresses once again that our conduct must nevertheless remain correct, that no notes may be taken which may not be inspected.

The younger officers and soldiers are showing a tendency towards the east presumably for two reasons:

1. We want to be on the right side because the Russians will win, no matter what.
2. We will live better under the Russians.

This gives the appearance of clinging to an illusion. At the moment this pro-Russian attitude is based on clever Soviet and clumsy Allied propaganda.

We must keep saying to the soldiers, "When the war is ended, you all rushed head over heels behind the British and American lines and now you want to go to the east? You are just being duped by Russian propaganda!"

We must say to them, "Be careful! If we throw ourselves into the Russians' arms, they won't have to pay a price for that."

The watchword must be, "Wait and see how things develop."

In the conferences held May 19 and 20, 1945, Jodl expresses the following views, "One must not say that one is specifically oriented towards the east or the west; that is politically wrong. One must be neutral.

"It will, however, be important for the Western Allies to know the strength of the Soviet forces drawn up behind the so-called demarcation line. According to our latest reports, the Soviet forces on the Russian western front, i.e. on the Soviet-

Allied demarcation line on the day of the capitulation, were as follows:

64 armies
3 Romanian armies
7 tank armies

together with:

491 rifle divisions
21 Romanian divisions
39 tank corps

In addition, there were:

7 cavalry corps
5 Romanian cavalry divisions
151 independent tank units
1 Romanian tank division

On the Allied side, there were approximately 120 motorized infantry or armored divisions.

Even taking into account the higher combat value of the Allied divisions, this is a ratio of about 4:1 in favor of the Soviets over the Western Allies.

Jodl issues a general directive: "Absolute neutrality, identical behavior towards the Russians and the Western Allies."

Thus all three Control Commissions—the American commanded by General Rooks, the British commanded by Brigadier Foord, and the Soviet Russian commanded by Major General Truskov—are given identical material concerning all military, political, and economic matters.

Jodl adds, "It is wrong to sell oneself. As a nation in the center, we are a factor which must be reckoned with. One must not decide prematurely, only when it is absolutely unavoidable. In our case, however, we must choose the side which will safeguard the German nation.

"After this there will be no civil life. The problems which

must be solved are too strong and pressing. Think politically—this must be hammered into all officers."

Paragraph 47 of the Military Disciplinary Code must be referred to whenever war crimes are mentioned.

"Can a subordinate be held responsible if he simply carries out the orders of his superior? The question is raised as to which law has moral superiority, the law which states that in war one does everything to ensure the victory of one's nation or the law which follows internationally concluded treaties that govern the conduct of war?"

In Jodl's view, one thing is sure, "Nothing we did that violated international treaties was done for reasons of hunger for power, but because Hitler considered it necessary to achieve victory.

"And in this case, should a soldier be expected to say, 'I will not carry out this order'?"

*   *   *

This concludes the personal diary entries and notes of the "last 30 days", which form the basis of this manuscript. Until May 23, 1945, the OKW continued to carry out its functions as part of the government of Grand Admiral Dönitz under the authority of the Allied and Soviet Russian Control Commissions and attempted to make its assigned contribution in the execution of the conditions of the capitulation and the reinstitution of law and order.

Its task ended, as did Dönitz's government, when the Grand Admiral and his staffs were placed under arrest by the Allies on the morning of May 23, 1945.

Documents

Excerpts from the War Diary of the Wehrmacht Operations Staff and Wehrmacht Reports from April 29–May 3, 1945

War Diary
April 29, 1945

Development of the Situation.

House to house fighting in the center of Berlin rages day and night.

0030 hours: General Jodl demands an immediate report from General Winter on the measures taken against the mutineers in Erding.

0340 hours: General Winter's report arrives; Radio Munich is broadcasting that the Führer has been killed.

0510 hours: General Winter is informed that the news is false; at this time there are still telephone communications with the Reich Chancellery.

The General [Jodl] expects the actions ordered against the treacherous gang in Erding to be carried out.

0735 hours: General Winter reports on the situation in Munich. The attitude of Ritter von Epp is unclear; he has been handed over the Security Service. The leader of the *putsch,* commander of the Interpreters Company, has escaped with his officers. There are some signs of the effects of the Munich events on troops at the front. Most energetic countermeasures are ensured.

1100 hours: The Grand Admiral calls to report that the enemy has established a bridgehead over the Elbe at Lauenburg. He believes that nothing more should be sent to Army Group Vistula and Twelfth Army High Command, but that efforts should be concentrated against the British on the Elbe. He calls for a joint cooperation.

1235 hours: Last conversation with Berlin (with Combat Commandant General Weidling), no longer with the Reich Chancellery.

1237 hours: General Heinrici reports that he has ordered General von Manteuffel to assume temporary command. General von Manteuffel reports that in this critical and decisive period he cannot relinquish his own command. Field Marshal Keitel therefore orders General von Tippelskirch to assume command of the Army Group immediately.

1250 hours: The radio communications balloon at Fürstenberg has been shot down by air attack.

1530 hours: Departure from the forestry station via headquarters of Twenty-first Army: Commander in Chief Tippelskirch initially unwilling to take over Army Group. The Commander in Chief of the OKW urgently reminds him of his duty; Tippelskirch understands the situation; he promises to devote himself completely to his task.

1600 hours: Situation report radioed to Reich Chancellery:
No reports from Ninth Army. Twelfth Army continues to push on to Berlin via Potsdam. Left wing of Twelfth Army and right wing of Army Group Vistula are conducting a successful defense. Army Group Vistula is trying to stop the enemy breakthrough on the line Liebenwalde–Lychen–Neubrandenburg–Anklam–Usedom–Wollin.

1900 hours: Departure from Neuroofen on forest trails to Dobbin.

1931 hours: Radio message from General Krebs and *Reichsleiter* Bormann for Field Marshal Keitel arrives. "Following rumors in foreign press of new treachery, the Führer expects that you will act with lightning speed and iron severity, allowing no favors." The Führer expects that Wenck, Schörner and others prove their loyalty to him by the most rapid relief action.

2028 hours: Advance oral, telex to follow, for Army Group Vistula:
"It is the mission of Army Group Vistula, while holding the southern and eastern front, to attack and destroy with all available forces the enemy who has broken through in the direction of Neubrandenburg. Report on execution of the assault by 2100 hours. Twenty-first Army High Command is to be committed on the right wing of the Army Group.

2300 hours: General Jodl receives the following radio message from the Führer in Dobbin:
"Report to me immediately:

1. Where are Wenck's leading elements?
2. When will they continue to attack?
3. Where is the Ninth Army?
4. In which direction will the Ninth Army break through?
5. Where are Holste's leading elements?"

2330 hours: Twelfth Army High Command first general staff officer (Ia) reports on the situation with Twelfth Army High Command and XXth Corps. Forced into the defensive on the entire front, the assault on Berlin is no longer possible, particularly as support from the Ninth Army can no longer be expected.

Threat to deep flanks and rear by American thrust on Coswig; impossibility of further attacks to the north greatly increasing. Resumption of American advance on entire western front probable due to their current conduct of operations. Army High Command requests immediate decision for future combat mission.

The decision was given over the telephone in advance of the following radio signal: "To Twelfth Army High Command: If Commander in Chief of the Twelfth Army is convinced, in full knowledge of the situation of his *XX AK* and despite the great ethical and historical responsibility imposed on us, that a continuation of the attack in direction of Berlin can not be executed, he should make preparations for the breakthrough to the north of XXth Corps, across the lower Havel. Report your consideration for this. Orders to execute the plan after approval by the Führer. Signed: Keitel."

Order concerning movement of forces from area between Ems and Elbe east of Hamburg.

Letter from General Winter to General Jodl requesting news of potential successor to the Führer should he fall.

Wehrmacht Report
April 29, 1945

Fanatical house to house fighting rages day and night in the center of Berlin. The brave garrison defends itself in the desperate struggle against incessant attacks by the Bolshevik masses. Despite this, a further enemy advance into certain suburbs could not be averted. Heavy street fighting is going on along *Potsdamer Strasse* and around *Belle Alliance Platz.* From Plötzensee the enemy has broken through to the Spree.

South of Berlin the Soviets threw fresh formations against our divisions attacking there; see saw fighting continues. Beelitz has been captured, and east of Werder communications with the defense district of Potsdam have been established. Assaults on the eastern flank of this advance northwest and southwest of Treuenbrietzen have been bloodily repulsed.

In the area of Mecklenburg and Pommern, the Soviet 5th Guards Division has been newly committed and has pushed our units back toward Templin and the chain of lakes between Lychen–Neubrandenburg and Anklam.

In northwest Germany there was heavy local fighting on the lower Ems, during which Leer was lost.

The British are forming a small bridgehead on the north bank of the Elbe under heavy artillery protection at Lauenburg, southeast of Hamburg. Reserves have launched a counterattack.

In Upper Swabia the enemy is pushing against the Memmingen–Augsburg line.

In Italy the enemy is trying to thwart the withdrawal of our divisions with heavy attacks northwest out of the Parma area and northwards out of their Po bridgeheads. At Piacenza and Verona intense battles with enemy advance elements are under way.

Yesterday, too, the Bolsheviks limited their actions in the

southern sector of the eastern front to local advances. From the area of Brünn they continued their breakthrough attempts and began their expected attack west of Mährisch–Ostrau. Austerlitz fell into enemy hands. Heavy fighting goes on with Soviet attacking forces which have broken through the front.

The brave defenders of *Breslau* beat off strong attacks on their western front inflicting losses on the enemy.

In the battle sector of *Bautzen–Meissen,* our forces continued to attack northwards. Kamenz and Königsbrück were retaken. The Soviets were thrown back with heavy losses.

Yesterday, after intense artillery preparation from the mainland, the enemy was able to gain a foothold on the eastern tip of the Frische Nehrung. Our forces had to concede a limited area to the enemy after fighting involving heavy losses on both sides.

There was weak enemy fighter plane activity yesterday over the entire Reich.

Continuing their fight against the enemy's resupply organization, our U-boats sank another eight fully laden freighters with 45,000 BRT (British Register Tons), three destroyers and two corvettes.

War Diary
May 3, 1945

Situation on the Fronts

In the capital of the Reich, the remnants of the brave garrison still keep up their heroic defense against the Bolsheviks.

In the early afternoon hours the headquarters relocates from Neustadt to Mürwik.

At 0400 hours, Field Marshal Keitel and General Jodl drive from Plön to Flensburg–Mürwik.

Grand Admiral Dönitz orders that Kiel will not be defended.

1000 hours: Conference with the Grand Admiral in Mürwik.

1120 hours: Order to Combat Commandant Schleswig, all available forces to be moved to the Kaiser Wilhelm Canal, which is to be defended.

On receiving reports of strengths and combat-effectiveness of troops on and to the north of the Kaiser Wilhelm Canal, it becomes evident that there is a general shortage of heavy weapons and, in some cases, also of small arms and anti-tank weapons.

1310 hours: Order to Combat Commandant Rendsburg that the city may not be given up. Bridges over the canal shall not be blown-up, however the canal is to be defended with all available means.

1350 hours: Order to the Flensburg *Kreisleiter* to organize orderly distribution of available supplies of clothing and food to the civilian population.

Midday: Conference with *Gauleiter* Terboven and the Commander in Chief of Norway, General Böhme. The results of the conference are sent to Army High Command Norway in a telex. They confirm that Commander in Chief Norway, in his

117

capacity as Wehrmacht Commander, is authorized to issue all military orders to Wehrmacht services and other organizations (except the police) as he sees fit during the current situation. Lieutenant Colonel de Maizière is flying to Kurland and East Prussia to communicate personally the Grand Admiral's aims and intentions on evacuation.

1453 hours: Radio message to Field Marshal Kesselring and General Winter. Field Marshal Kesselring is authorized to conclude a ceasefire with the 6th American Army Group for the troops on the western front between the Bohemian forest and the upper Inn. In so doing, he must establish how far to the east the Anglo-Americans intend to advance. Thus the basis for negotiating the rescue of the Army Groups Löhr, Rendulic and Schörner must be established. The Seventh Army will be assigned to Schörner.

1930 hours: Radio message to Army East Prussia and Army Group Kurland. The changed military situation in the Reich requires the accelerated evacuation of numerous units from East and West Prussia and from Kurland.

The conduct of operations of the Army East Prussia and the Army Group Kurland will conform with this requirement.

Personnel of those units being evacuated are to embark with light infantry weapons. All other materiel, including horses, is to be left behind and destroyed. The Army Group Kurland is given operational freedom to withdraw the main front line into planned bridgeheads around the ports of Libau and Windau.

The Navy will move all available means of transport to East Prussia and Kurland.

On May 3, 1945 Admiral von Friedeburg established liaison with Marshal Montgomery.

Wehrmacht Report
May 3, 1945

In the capital of the Reich, the remnants of the brave garrison still keep up their heroic defense against the Bolsheviks in isolated blocks of houses and in the government quarter.

During heavy local fighting, the situation in northwestern Germany between the Ems and lower Weser remained generally unchanged. The British advanced on both sides of the Elbe–Trave Canal from the area of Mölln toward Lübeck and took the city. Advance enemy elements reached Bad Segeberg and the area northwest of Plön. The Americans, advancing north and northwest out of Schwerin, pushed to the coast at Wismar and into the Gadebusch area.

In Mecklenburg our troops generally held the line from the Plauer Lake to Rostock against heavy Bolshevik attacks.

In Bavaria the Americans have pushed back our greatly reduced forces to the Inn. The superior enemy forces overwhelmed the defenders of Munich. The enemy has achieved deep penetration on both sides of the Würm Lake and have established a bridgehead on the east bank of the Inn south of Rosenheim. Street fighting in Bregenz on Lake Constance.

On the western Alps front our troops are fighting their way back to the northeast under most difficult conditions. Enemy pressure continues at the northern end of Lake Garda. Enemy forces advancing on the Alpine foothills have forced their way into Castelfranco and Bassano. In Istria the garrison of Fiume is holding out against concentric enemy attacks. On the Croatian eastern front our troops also continue to hold their positions against numerous attacks by strong guerrilla forces.

On the eastern front the Bolsheviks continued their attempted breakthrough in the Nikolsburg sector. Apart from local successes they failed. Northeast of Brünn, the enemy has been able to enlarge his penetration and has taken Wischau after heavy fighting. Southwest of Mährisch–Ostrau, the Soviet penetration was checked by an immediate counter-attacks after a gain of a few kilometers.

Heavy defensive fighting continues on the Frische Nehrung. From Kurland only local fighting is reported.

The enemy air forces carried out many low-flying attacks, particularly in the north German area, and continued their terror attacks against the civilian population.

The High Command of the Armed Forces further announces the following: "The High Command of the Armed Forces has declared the naval bases of Kiel and Flensburg open cities and ordered that they are not to be defended."

In addition to the Wehrmacht report, the military informed us: On Wednesday, "In the capital of the Reich, the Soviets once more applied the full weight of their war materiel to break the resistance of the fanatically fighting garrison. Guns and rocket launchers fired incessantly; bombs rained down continuously and the rattling of machine guns was ceaseless. Enemy tanks and storm battalions edged their way forward, step by step, through the collapsing houses of the old city. Exploding charges ripped bunkers and underground railway shafts. Their ruins buried attacker and defender alike. In the government quarter, the heroes of Berlin are fulfilling the Führer's last will and testament with their last strength."

Numerous independent pockets of resistance, fighting alone, still cause the enemy considerable difficulties.

Southwest and west of Berlin, our troops are fighting their way back to the northwest after having received the Ninth Army which broke out of enemy encirclement. They beat off heavy flank attacks and held open the connecting communications corridor by means of their tough resistance at Brandenburg and Rathenow.

The main effort of the Bolshevik attacks lay in Mecklenburg. Here the enemy pushed westward between the Plauer Lake and the Bay of Mecklenburg with numerous strong assault wedges. Most of their assaults collapsed. Soviet forces advancing on a broad front are being met by strong British forces from the Mölln–Lübeck area. Advance tank forces made contact with the Bolsheviks near Grabow and Wismar. On Thursday, a second British wedge driving north into the upper Trave area, reached the Bad–Segeberg–Plön line and advanced through the undefended Kiel area with its forward elements up to the area of Eckernförde. Our planes covered our continued disengagement movement against continuous low-flying British fighter attacks. Between Hamburg and Leer, the British carried out only local attacks near Stade, Oldenburg and the area of the Ems estuary. Significant gains were denied them.

In the southern defensive area between Munich and Brünn, Dresden and St. Pölten, the enemy pushed our much reduced forces further back in the Alpine foothills and in Lower Bavaria. In the Lake Constance area and at Bregenz, heavy fighting has broken out with the enemy pushing towards the Swiss border and the Arlberg pass.

Anglo-American efforts launched from Füssen and Partenkirchen to cross the watershed between the Isar and the Inn failed, while east of Munich enemy tank units formed a bridgehead at Rosenheim. Following heavy street fighting in Munich, elements of the Seventh U.S. Army thus relieved, have joined the assault on the Inn line. Strong enemy forces remain tied down in the Passau area, however, so that only light forces were able to reconnoiter along the courage of the Danube valley.

In the Bohemian Forest and the Lausitz, along the Sudetes Mountains hills and near Brünn, there was only local fighting. In the Lausitz our troops enlarged yesterday's penetrations into the main enemy battle positions. The garrison of Breslau again repulsed strong Soviet attacks. In Mährisch–Ostrau and on both sides of Brünn, our forces frustrated powerful Bolshevik breakthrough attempts at Wittkowitz, Wischau, Brünn and Nikolsburg.

Maps and the Instruments of Capitulation

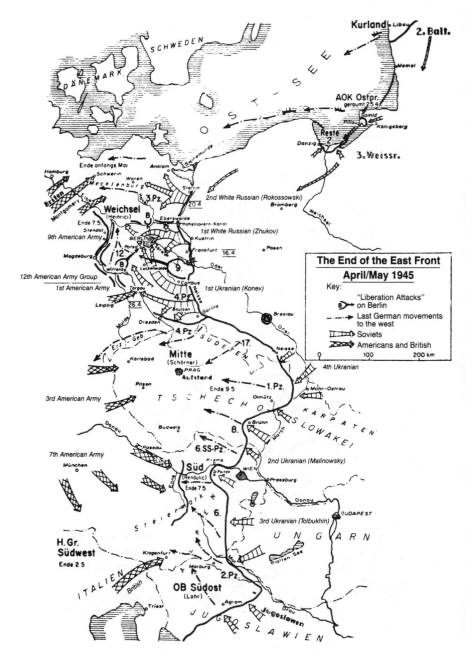

The End of the Eastern Front April/May 1945

125

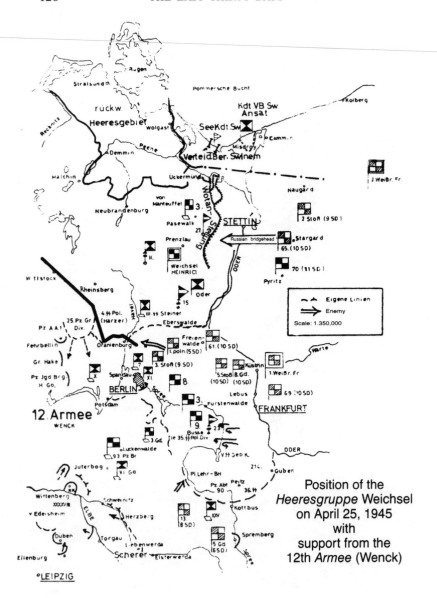

Position of the
Heeresgruppe Weichsel
on April 25, 1945
with
support from the
12th *Armee* (Wenck)

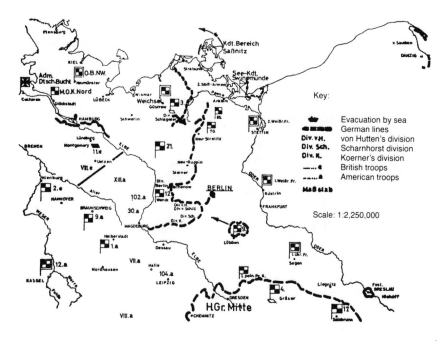

**Situation on the Eastern and Western Fronts on
April 30, 1945 (Hitler's suicide in Berlin).**

The position of German divisions at the time of the capitulation at Rheims (May 7, 1945). Each dot represents a division or a divisional group. Kurland, Holland and Norway are not included. (From OKW files.)

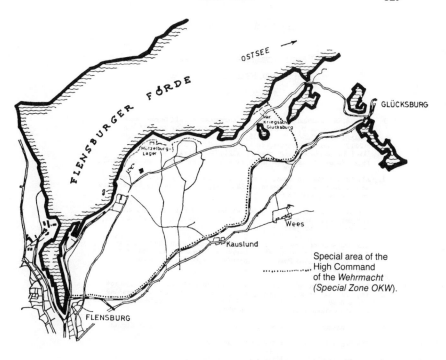

Special area of the
High Command
of the *Wehrmacht*
(Special Zone OKW).

The Mürwik Enclave
May 5–23, 1945

Instrument of Surrender

of

All German armed forces in HOLLAND, in

northwest Germany including all islands,

and in DENMARK.

1. The German Command agrees to the surrender of all German armed
   forces in HOLLAND, in northwest GERMANY including the FRISIAN
   ISLANDS and HELIGOLAND and all other islands, in SCHLESWIG-
   HOLSTEIN, and in DENMARK, to the C.-in-C. 21 Army Group.
   This to include all naval ships in these areas.
   These forces to lay down their arms and to surrender unconditionally.

2. All hostilities on land, on sea, or in the air by German forces
   in the above areas to cease at 0800 hrs. British Double Summer Time
   on Saturday 5 May 1945.

3. The German command to carry out at once, and without argument or
   comment, all further orders that will be issued by the Allied
   Powers on any subject.

4. Disobedience of orders, or failure to comply with them, will be
   regarded as a breach of these surrender terms and will be dealt
   with by the Allied Powers in accordance with the accepted laws
   and usages of war.

5. This instrument of surrender is independent of, without prejudice
   to, and will be superseded by any general instrument of surrender
   imposed by or on behalf of the Allied Powers and applicable to Germany
   and the German armed forces as a whole.

6. This instrument of surrender is written in English and in German.

   The English version is the authentic text.

7. The decision of the Allied Powers will be final if any doubt or
   dispute arises as to the meaning or interpretation of the surrender
   terms.

[handwritten signatures]

B. L. Montgomery
Field-Marshal

4 May 1945
1830 hrs.

Armistice with the British on May 5, 1945 at Lüneburg.

Kapitulations-Urkunde

der gesamten deutschen Streitkräfte in Holland, in Nordwest-deutschland einschließlich aller Inseln und in Dänemark.

1. Das Oberkommando der deutschen Wehrmacht erklärt sich einverstanden mit der Übergabe sämtlicher deutscher Streitkräfte in Holland, in Nordwest-Deutschland einschl. der Fries. Inseln und Helgoland und allen anderen Inseln, in Schleswig-Holstein und in Dänemark an den Oberbefehlshaber der 21. Heeresgruppe. Dieses schließt alle Schiffe in diesen Zonen ein. Diese Streitkräfte haben die Waffen zu strecken und sich bedingungslos zu ergeben.

2. Alle Kampfhandlungen auf dem Lande, zur See und in der Luft durch deutsche Streitkräfte in den vorgenannten Gebieten sind um 08.00 Uhr vormittags doppelte britische Sommerzeit am Sonnabend, den 5. Mai 1945, einzustellen.

3. Die betreffenden deutschen Befehlsstellen haben sofort und ohne Widerrede oder Kommentar alle weiteren Befehle auszuführen, welche durch die alliierten Mächte in jedweder Sache erteilt werden.

4. Ungehorsam in Bezug auf Befehle oder Ermangelungen in deren Ausführung werden als Bruch dieser Übergabebedingungen angesehen und werden von den alliierten Mächten laut den anerkannten Rechten und Kriegsgebräuchen behandelt.

5. Diese Übergabebedingungen sind unabhängig von, ohne Vorbehalt auf und werden überholt durch irgendwelche allgem. Übergabebedingungen, welche durch oder im Auftrage der alliierten Mächte gestellt werden in Bezug auf Deutschland und den deutschen Streitkräften im ganzen.

6. Der Wortlaut dieser Kapitulationsurkunde ist engl. und in deutscher Sprache aufgestellt. Der engl. Text ist der maßgebende.

7. Sollten sich irgendwelche Zweifel oder Dispute bezüglich der Auslegung oder Deutung der Übergabebedingungen ergeben, so ist die Entscheidung der alliierten Mächte die endgültige.

B. L. Montgomery	v. Friedeburg
Feldmarschall	Kinzel
	G. Wagner
4. Mai 1945	Poleck
18.30 Uhr	Friedel

Armistice with the British on May 5, 1945 at Lüneburg (German text).

(Seekriegsleitung B Nr. 1. Skl. 1059/45 GKdos. Militärgeschichtliches Forschungsamt, Freiburg.)

Hauptquartier,den 6. Mai 1945.

Ich bevollmächtige Generaloberst   J o d l ,

Chef des Wehrmachtführungsstabes im Oberkommando

der Wehrmacht, zum Abschluss eines Waffenstill-

standsabkommens mit dem Hauptquartier des Generals

E i s e n h o w e r .

GroßadmiraI.

Power of Attorney for General Jodl.

Only this text in English is authoritative

ACT OF MILITARY SURRENDER

1.   We the undersigned, acting by authority
of the German High Command, hereby surrender
unconditionally to the Supreme Commander, Allied
Expeditionary Force and simultaneously to the
Soviet High Command all forces on land, sea, and in
the air who are at this date under German control.

2.   The German High Command will at once
issue orders to all German military, naval and
air authorities and to all forces under German
control to cease active operations at 2301 hours
Central European time on 8 May   and to
remain in the positions occupied at that time. No
ship, vessel, or aircraft is to be scuttled, or any
damage done to their hull, machinery or equipment.

3.   The German High Command will at once
issue to the appropriate commanders, and ensure
the carrying out of any further orders issued by
the Supreme Commander, Allied Expeditionary Force
and by the Soviet High Command.

4.   This act of military surrender is without
prejudice to, and will be superseded by any
general instrument of surrender imposed by, or
on behalf of the United Nations and applicable
to GERMANY and the German armed forces as a whole.

5. In the event of the German High Command
or any of the forces under their control failing
to act in accordance with this Act of Surrender,
the Supreme Commander, Allied Expeditionary Force
and the Soviet High Command will take such punitive
or other action as they deem appropriate.

Signed at *Rheims at 0241* on the 7th day of May, 1945.
France

On behalf of the German High Command.

[signature: Jodl]

IN THE PRESENCE OF

On behalf of the Supreme Commander,
Allied Expeditionary Force.

[signature: W. B. Smith]

On behalf of the Soviet
High Command.

[signature]

[signature] -2-

Major General, French Army
(Witness)

Act of Military Surrender with the U.S. Forces on May 7, 1945 at Rheims, France.

Urkunde über die militärische Kapitulation (Reims 7. Mai 1945)

1. Der Unterzeichnete, handelnd im Namen des deutschen Oberkommandos, erklärt hiermit die bedingungslose Kapitulation aller Streitkräfte zu Lande, zu Wasser und in der Luft, welche sich in diesem Augenblick unter deutscher Kontrolle befinden, gegenüber dem Obersten Befehlshaber der Alliierten Expeditionsstreitkräfte und gleichzeitig gegenüber dem Oberkommando der Sowjettruppen.

2. Das deutsche Oberkommando wird sofort an alle deutschen Kommandostellen der Land-, See- und Luftstreitkräfte und an alle unter deutscher Kontrolle stehenden Streitkräfte Befehle erteilen, Kampfhandlungen um 23 Uhr 1 mitteleuropäischer Zeit am 8. Mai einzustellen und in den zu dieser Zeit besetzten Stellungen zu verbleiben. Kein Schiff, kein Flugzeug oder Luftschiff darf unbrauchbar gemacht, noch darf dem Schiff- oder Flugkörper, dem maschinellen Teil oder der Ausrüstung irgend eine Beschädigung zugefügt werden.

3. Das deutsche Oberkommando wird sich sofort mit den in Betracht kommenden Befehlshabern in Verbindung setzen und die Ausführung irgendwelcher weiterer Anordnungen sicherstellen, die von dem Obersten Befehlshaber der Alliierten Expeditionsstreitkräfte und von dem Oberkommando der Sowjettruppen erlassen werden.

4. Die Urkunde militärischer Übergabe präjudiziert nicht ihre Ersetzung durch ein allgemeines Kapitulationsinstrument, das von und im Namen der Vereinten Nationen Deutschland und den deutschen Streitkräften in ihrer Gesamtheit auferlegt wird.

5. Falls das deutsche Oberkommando oder irgendwelche unter seiner Kontrolle stehenden Streitkräfte nicht entsprechend

dieser Kapitulationsurkunde handeln, werden der Oberste Befehlshaber der Alliierten Expeditionsstreitkräfte und das Oberkommando der Sowjettruppen die ihnen geeignet erscheinenden Strafmaßnahmen ergreifen oder in anderer Weise vorgehen.

Gezeichnet zu Reims um 2 Uhr 41 am 7. Tage des Mai 1945. Frankreich.

Im Namen des deutschen Oberkommandos
Jodl

In Gegenwart von:
Im Namen d. Obersten Befehlshabers d. Alliierten Expeditionsstreitkräfte
W. B. Smith

Im Namen des Oberkommandos der Sowjettruppen
Sousloparov

F. Sevez
Generalmajor der französischen Armee
(Zeuge)

Act of Military Surrender with the U.S. Forces on May 7, 1945 at Rheims, France (German text).

Der Oberste Befehlshaber
der Wehrmacht

Hauptquartier, den **7.**5.45.

/Bitte in der Antwort vorstehendes
Geschäftszeichen, das Datum und
kurzen Inhalt anzugeben./

ICH BEVOLLMÄCHTIGE

GENERALFELDMARSCHALL   K E I T E L

ALS CHEF DES OBERKOMMANDOS DER

WEHRMACHT UND ZUGLEICH ALS OBER-

BEFEHLSHABER DES HEERES,

GENERALADMIRAL VON FRIEDEBURG

ALS OBERBEFEHLSHABER DER KRIEGSMARINE,

GENERALOBERST   S T U M P F

ALS VERTRETER DES OBERBEFEHLSHABERS

DER LUFTWAFFE

ZUR RATIFIZIERUNG DER BEDINGUNGSLÖSEN

KAPITULATION DER DEUTSCHEN STREITKRÄFTE GEGEN-

ÜBER DEM OBERBEFEHLSHABER DER ALLIIERTEN

EXPEDITIONSSTREITKRÄFTE UND DEM SOWJET-OBER-

KOMMANDO.

DÖNITZ

GROßADMIRAL.

Siegel.

Верно: cannby (cocnotauui)

Grand Admiral Dönitz's order authorizing Field Marshal Keitel, Admiral von Friedeburg and General Stumpff to surrender to the Allied Expeditionary Force and the Soviet High Command.

ACT OF MILITARY SURRENDER

1.   We the undersigned, acting by authority
of the German High Command, hereby surrender
unconditionally to the Supreme Commander, Allied
Expeditionary Force and simultaneously to the
Supreme High Command of the Red Army all forces
on land, at sea, and in the air who are at this
date under German control.

2.   The German High Command will at once
issue orders to all German military, naval and
air authorities and to all forces under German
control to cease active operations at 2301 hours
Central European time on 8th May 1945, to remain
in the positions occupied at that time and to
disarm completely, handing over their weapons and
equipment to the local allied commanders or officers
designated by Representatives of the Allied Supreme
Commands.   No ship, vessel, or aircraft is to be
scuttled, or any damage done to their hull,
machinery or equipment, and also to machines of all
kinds, armament, apparatus, and all the technical
means of prosecution of war in general.

3. The German High Command will at once issue to the appropriate commanders, and ensure the carrying out of any further orders issued by the Supreme Commander, Allied Expeditionary Force and by the Supreme High Command of the Red Army.

4. This act of military surrender is without prejudice to, and will be superseded by any general instrument of surrender imposed by, or on behalf of the United Nations and applicable to GERMANY and the German armed forces as a whole.

5. In the event of the German High Command or any of the forces under their control failing to act in accordance with this Act of Surrender, the Supreme Commander, Allied Expeditionary Force and the Supreme High Command of the Red Army will take such punitive or other action as they deem appropriate.

6. This Act is drawn up in the English, Russian and German languages. The English and Russian are the only authentic texts.

Signed at *Berlin* on the *8.* day of May, 1945

[signatures]

On behalf of the German High Command

- -

IN THE PRESENCE OF:

[signature]

On behalf of the
Supreme Commander
Allied Expeditionary Force

On behalf of the
Supreme High Command of the
Red Army

At the signing also were present as witnesses:

[signature]

General Commanding in Chief
First French Army

[signature]

General, Commanding
United States Strategic Air Forces

Act of Military Surrender with Allied Forces and the Red Army on May 8, 1945 at Berlin.

АКТ О ВОЕННОЙ КАПИТУЛЯЦИИ.

1. Мы, нижеподписавшиеся, действуя от имени Германского Верховного Командования, соглашаемся на безоговорочную капитуляцию всех наших вооруженных сил на суше, на море и в воздухе, а также всех сил, находящихся в настоящее время под немецким командованием, - Верховному Главнокомандованию Красной Армии и одновременно Верховному Командованию Союзных Экспедиционных сил.

2. Германское Верховное командование немедленно издает приказы всем немецким командующим сухопутными, морскими и воздушными силами и всем силам, находящимся под германским командованием, прекратить военные действия в 23-01 час по Центрально-Европейскому времени 8 мая 1945 года, остаться на своих местах, где они находятся в это время, и полностью разоружиться, передав все их оружие и военное имущество местным союзным командующим или офицерам, выделенным представителями Союзных Верховных Командований, не разрушать и не причинять никаких повреждений пароходам, судам и самолетам, их двигателям, корпусам и оборудованию, а также машинам, вооружению, аппаратам и всем вообще военно-техническим средствам ведения войны.

3. Германское Верховное Командование немедленно выделит соответствующих командиров и обеспечит выполнение всех дальнейших приказов,изданных Верховным Главнокомандованием Красной Армии и Верховным Командованием Союзных Экспедиционных сил.

4. Этот акт не будет являться препятствием к замене его другим генеральным документом о капитуляции,заключенным Об'единенными Нациями или от их имени,применимым к Германии и германским вооруженным силам в целом.

5. В случае, если немецкое Верховное Командование или какие-либо вооруженные силы,находящиеся под его командованием, не будут действовать в соответствии с этим актом о капитуляции, Верховное Командование Красной Армии,а также Верховное Командование Союзных Экспедиционных сил, предпримут такие карательные меры, или другие действия, которые они сочтут необходимыми.

6. Этот акт составлен на английском, русском и немецком языках. Только английский и русский тексты являются аутентичными.

Подписано 8 мая 1945 года в гор. БЕРЛИНЕ.

От имени Германского Верховного Командования:

В присутствии:

По уполномочию Верховного
Командующего Экспедиционными
силами Союзников
ГЛАВНОГО МАРШАЛА АВИАЦИИ
ТЕДДЕРА

По уполномочию Верховного
Главнокомандования Красной
Армии
МАРШАЛА СОВЕТСКОГО СОЮЗА
Г.ЖУКОВА

При подписании также присутствовали в качестве свидетелей:

Командующий Стратегическими
Воздушными силами США
ГЕНЕРАЛ
СПААТС

Главнокомандующий Французской
Армией
ГЕНЕРАЛ ДЕЛАТР
де ТАССИНЬИ

**Act of Military Surrender with Allied Forces and the Red Army on
May 8, 1945 at Berlin (Russian text).**

KAPITULATIONSERKLAERUNG.

1. Wir, die hier Unterzeichneten, handelnd in Vollmacht fuer und im Namen des Oberkommandos der Deutschen Wehrmacht, erklaeren hiermit die bedingungslose Kapitulation aller am gegenwaertigen Zeitpunkt unter deutschem Befehl stehenden oder von Deutschland beherrschten Streitkraefte auf dem Lande, auf der See und in der Luft gleichzeitig gegenueber dem Obersten Befehlshaber der Alliierten Expeditions Streitkraefte und dem Oberkommando der Roten Armee.

2. Das Oberkommando der Deutschen Wehrmacht wird unverzueglich allen Behoerden der deutschen Land-,See- und Luftstreitkraefte und allen von Deutschland beherrschten Streitkraeften den Befehl geben, die Kampfhandlungen um 2301 Uhr Mitteleuropaeischer Zeit am 8 Mai einzustellen und in den Stellungen zu verbleiben, die sie an diesem Zeitpunkt innehaben und sich vollstaendig zu entwaffnen, indem sie Waffen und Geraete an die oertlichen Alliierten Befehlshaber beziehungsweise an die von den Alliierten Vertretern zu bestimmenden Offiziere abliefern. Kein Schiff, Boot oder Flugzeug irgendeiner Art darf versenkt werden, noch duerfen Schiffsruempfe, maschinelle Einrichtungen, Ausruestungsgegenstaende, Maschinen irgendwelcher Art, Waffen, Apparaturen, technische Gegenstaende, die Kriegszwecken im Allgemeinen dienlich sein koennen, beschaedigt werden.

3. Das Oberkommando der Deutschen Wehrmacht wird unverzueglich den zustaendigen Befehlshabern alle von dem Obersten Befehlshaber der Alliierten Expeditions Streitkraefte und dem Oberkommando der Roten Armee erlassenen zusaetzlichen Befehle weitergeben und deren Durchfuehrung sicherstellen.

4. Diese Kapitulationserklaerung ist ohne Praejudiz fuer irgendwelche an ihre Stelle tretenden allgemeinen Kapitulationsbestimmungen, die durch die Vereinten Nationen und in deren Namen Deutschland und der Deutschen Wehrmacht auferlegt werden moegen.

5. Falls das Oberkommando der Deutschen Wehrmacht oder irgendwelche ihm unterstehende oder von ihm beherrschte Streitkraefte es versaeumen sollen, sich gemaess den Bestimmungen dieser Kapitulations-Erklaerung zu verhalten,

werden der Oberste Befehlshaber der Alliierten Expeditions
Streitkraefte und das Oberkommando der Roten Armee alle
diejenigen Straf- und anderen Massnahmen ergreifen, die sie
als zweckmaessig erachten.

    6.   Diese Erklaerung ist in englischer, russischer und
deutscher Sprache abgefasst. Allein massgebend sind die
englische und die russische Fassung.

Unterzeichnet zu *Berlin*   am   *8*   Mai 1945

Fuer das Oberkommando der Deutschen Wehrmacht.

In Gegenwart von:

Fuer den Obersten Befehlshaber
der Alliierten Expeditions-
Streitkraefte.

Fuer das Oberkommando
der Roten Armee

Bei der Unterzeichnung waren als Zeugen
auch zugegen:

General, Oberstkommandierender
der Ersten Franzoesischen Armee

Kommandierender General
der Strategischen
Luftstreitkraefte der
Vereinigten Staaten

**Act of Military Surrender with Allied Forces and the Red Army on
May 8, 1945 at Berlin (German text).**

PART TWO

The Battle for Berlin

THE ADVANCE TO THE ODER

By mid-April 1945, the Soviets had closed to the Neisse and Oder line with the First Ukrainian Front* under Marshal Konev and the First Belorussian Front commanded by Marshal Rokossovsky.

The Soviet army groups were assembled in the following staging areas: the First Ukrainian Front between Görlitz and Guben on the Neisse; the First Belorussian Front with the three tank armies and eight to ten infantry armies adjacent with the main forces between Fürstenberg and Schwedt on the Oder. The main concentration was located near Küstrin. The Second Belorussian Front, with one tank and four to five infantry armies, was located between Schwedt and the Baltic coast.

On the German side stood Army Group Center, commanded by Field Marshal Schörner from the Sudetes Mountains to the lower Neisse; and, along the Oder to the Baltic at Swinemünde, the Army Group Vistula commanded by General Heinrici.

The formations employed were, beginning from the right wing of the Army Group Vistula: the Ninth Army commanded

---

*A Front is equivalent to an Army Group.

by Lieutenant General Busse with the Vth SS Mountain Corps, XIth SS Corps and CI Corps. Next in line were the Third Panzer Army, commanded by General von Manteuffel, with the XLVIth Panzer Corps, SS Corps *Oder,* XXXIInd Corps, and east of Swinemünde, the 3rd Naval Division.

The reserves available to the Army Group Vistula were concentrated mainly behind the center and left wing of the Ninth Army and the right wing of the Third Panzer Army. Specifically, these reserves were: LVIth Panzer Corps, 20th Panzer Division, 9th Airborne Division, Panzer Division *Müncheberg,* 25th Panzergrenadier Division, 18th Panzergrenadier Division, SS Panzergrenadier Division *Nordland* and SS Panzergrenadier Division *Nederland.*

The German forces were much inferior in personnel and materiel (particularly in artillery and tanks) in comparison with the Soviet assault formations ranged in depth east of the Oder. As early as January 31, 1945, light Soviet motorized units had pushed forward past Wriezen, north of Berlin. That was the first occasion on which the tank alarm had been sounded in Berlin. Having outpaced their main forces, these Russian advance forces could be turned back.

By the beginning of April 1945, the front, which followed the Oder river, had been consolidated on the German side. That occurred after the Ninth Army had repeatedly attempted without success to eliminate the Soviet bridgehead across the Oder at Küstrin. The bridgehead was to serve as a springboard for future Soviet operations.

THE BERLIN DEFENSE ZONE

Command in the Defense Zone

The command in the Defense Zone was held consecutively by the commander in Defense District III, General von Kortzfleisch, General Ritter von Hauenschild, and General Reymann. The latter separated the Defense District Command and

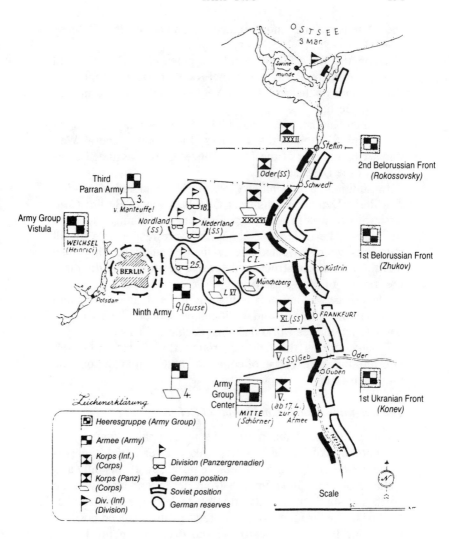

The Oder Front in mid-April 1945.

the Defense Zone and retained command of the Defense Zone.*

When the Russians stood at the gates of Berlin, General Reymann was replaced by Colonel Kaether. He was appointed Commander of the Army Group Spree, a blocking formation south of Berlin.

Colonel Kaether's command lasted only two days.

On April 23, on Hitler's orders, Lieutenant General Weidling, Commander of the LVIth Panzer Corps, assumed command of the Defense Zone.

In addition to the military organs of command, *Gauleiter* and Reich Defense Commissar Goebbels was in Berlin; *Gauleiter* Stürtz was in Mark Brandenburg performing the same functions. The Defense Commissars were responsible for all measures which affected the civilian population. They also had the task of constructing defensive positions and directing the training of the *Volkssturm*.

Thus there was not only a dualism in the chain of command between the military and political personnel; the two high party functionaries worked against each other as well.

Finally, during the fighting around Berlin, Hitler himself interfered in the exercise of command both within and outside the Reich capital.

The Defensive Positions and Means of Defense

Due to a lack of manpower, the topographical features on the outskirts of Berlin—forests, lakes, rivers, and canals—could not be exploited for defensive purposes. It was only at a distance of about 30 kilometers from Berlin, and mainly to the north and south of the city, that obstacles were constructed. East of Berlin, around Erkner-Tiefensee, an advanced position was built. Later on, due to the speed of the enemy breakthrough, this position could not be manned in time.

---

*The Reich was divided into Wehrkreise (Defense Districts) which generally coincided with the states or, in the case of Prussia, with the provinces.

The Berlin Defense Zone was divided into eight sectors labelled A through H. Each sector was commanded by a sector commander who operated with the authority of a divisional commander. The majority of these sector commanders had no front line experience as they were drawn mainly from the Replacement Army and the Zone of the Interior.

The first defensive position was located along the inner periphery of the city. It was reinforced to the east and west of the city by secondary positions to its rear. In the inner city, the 35 kilometer long circular railway was integrated into the defensive system. The inner combat ring was delineated by the Landwehr Canal and the Spree River. In this scheme, the sector from Wilhelmstrasse to the Reich Chancellery was designated the "Citadel."

The antiaircraft towers "Zoo," "Humboldthain," and "Friedrichshain" could be described as bastions of the defensive system. Although completely surrounded, they held out to the last against all assaults.

The towers served as antiaircraft strong points as well as large air raid shelters for the populace. In addition to their garrisons, they could accommodate up to 40,000 people. The towers had their own power and water supplies and efficient stocks of ammunition and food. During the fighting, they held well over the planned numbers of wounded and civilians.

The antiaircraft artillery of these towers participated continuously in ground combat.

Apart from the construction of defensive positions (as far as available manpower allowed), measures were taken to organize for regular house to house fighting.

The tunnels of the subway could be used by friend and foe alike for underground movements, and this occurred in the course of the fighting. During the battle for Berlin, various subway tunnels in the city center were demolished. This resulted in extensive underground flooding. Although almost all bridges and viaducts were prepared for demolition, a considerable number were saved from destruction. Statistics show that after the fighting ended, 59 out of a total of 229 bridges were completely intact. Essential manufacturing and supply plants were crippled but not destroyed. The construction of a cable and radio communication network, so vital to conducting a successful defense, was not possible due to lack of the necessary signals units and mobile materiel. Command of combat operations relied on the local telephone system. The defense buildup was provisional in all respects. Due to a lack of manpower and materiel, it was impossible to transform a metropolis the size of Berlin into a fortress within a few weeks.

The Strength and Organization of Local Defense Forces

Deployed in the Defense Zone were a variety of forces: stationary and antiaircraft artillery, *Alarmeinheiten* (emergency combat units), *Ersatzeinheiten* (Replacement Army units), army schools, *Landesschützen* (national guard), *Werkschutz* (Factory Protection units), *Postschutz* (Postal Protection units), *Panzervernichtungseinheiten* (Tank Destroyer units), Waffen-SS units, regular SS units, *Volkssturm*, and Hitler Youth units.

The stationary artillery consisted of light and heavy batteries, grouped together into weak regiments. Usually at least one regiment was allocated to each defense sector. The guns were almost all of foreign manufacture. The ammunition supply was therefor low, 20–30 rounds per gun being the norm. Most of the artillery was stationary; most regiments did not have even one tractor available. In the majority of cases, the battery commanders and gun crews were not artillery men. Only a few batteries had cable and radio communications. Where field and antiaircraft batteries were grouped together, an ad hoc system of transmitting orders could be organized using telephone and radio, supplemented by runners.

For antiaircraft defense the 1st Antiaircraft Division, commanded by Brigadier General Sydow, was deployed. His command post was located in the smaller of the two "Zoo" antiaircraft towers, and was referred to as the *Flakleitstand* (antiaircraft fire direction center). The division had four antiaircraft artillery regiments with pieces ranging from 20mm to 128mm in caliber. Each regiment had about four battalions.

The heart of the antiaircraft defenses were the above-mentioned antiaircraft towers "Zoo," "Friedrichshain," and "Humboldthain." Their armament varied. The "Zoo" tower, for example, had four twin 128mm guns and twelve 20mm guns. There was an adequate supply of ammunition. The barrage fire batteries used older German and foreign antiaircraft guns. Other stationary antiaircraft batteries were employed to strengthen the outer defenses.

The term *Alarmeinheiten* (emergency combat units) was first used in Russia in the winter of 1941–42. Stragglers, convalescents, headquarters staff personnel, logistical units and other duty stations were then, as now, combined and deployed in platoons, companies and battalions. Their combat-effectiveness and morale were low.

Even the few Replacement Army units available in Berlin had almost no combat experience.

The members of the Army School, Ammunition Technicians School and Armorer's School who were employed as compact units with their students had a certain combat-effectiveness.

In contrast, the *Landesschützeneinheiten* (national guard units), made up of older soldiers not fit for field service and equipped with captured rifles, could only be used to guard installations and camps.

The *Werkschutz* and *Postschutz* units, made up of the members of the large industrial plants, had only limited combat-effectiveness.

Panzerzerstöreinheiten (Tank Destroyer units) were intended to be used specifically in an anti-tank role.

The Waffen-SS had a special status. It had the mission of protecting the Reich Chancellery ("Citadel") and the command of the center of the city. It was in brigade strength and commanded by SS *Brigadeführer* [General] Mohnke. The SS troops were well-equipped and well-armed. They were characterized by high combat morale and therefore combat effectiveness.

Small units of the regular SS were employed in various defense sectors.

The *Volkssturm* and Hitler Youth formed the majority of the local defenders.*

The *Volkssturm* numbered about 60,000 men in about 90 battalions of varying strengths.

They could be compared to a kind of national guard. The *Volkssturm* units were composed of males of all age levels from boys to 60-year-olds, but mainly from the more senior age groups. The Nazi Party appointed the unit commanders who were either soldiers or party functionaries. Attempts to give military training in evening and weekend courses were often totally inadequate owing to a lack of weapons, ammunition and equipment.

The available weapons were mostly captured from the enemy. Among these were bazookas, but they remained mostly unused due to a lack of training.

Although one can scarcely consider the *Volkssturm* combateffective, some individual companies and battalions put up a brave resistance.

The Hitler Youth was not spared combat. They served in the *Volkssturm,* in the antiaircraft units as auxiliaries, and in independent Hitler Youth battalions. Some of the battalions of fifteen- and sixteen-year-olds formed the "Axmann Brigade"** which was supposed to hunt Soviet tanks with bazookas in the Bad Freienwalde area east of Berlin. Following protests by the general officer commanding the LVIth Panzer Corps General Weidling, Axmann realized the senselessness of setting these scarcely trained boys against a superior and merciless enemy and withdrew the order for their deployment. Unfortuntely, before this order could be rescinded, many members of the Hitler Youth were killed, wounded or captured.

Substantial parts of the Hitler Youth were in action to the

---

*The *Volkssturm* was a creation of the Nazi party, and was not an organic part of the Wehrmacht. Called up in autumn 1944, its forces could not be considered combat troops.

**Artur Axmann was the Reich Youth Leader.

west of Berlin in the Pichelsdorf sector and at the radio tower, where they bravely defended a bridgehead to the end.

Military and Civilian Supply and The Civilian Population

In the military sector, the supply of ammunition was so inadequate that the defenders suffered chronic ammunition shortages. The three large depots for German ammunition which were located in the outer suburbs fell into enemy hands shortly after the LVIth Panzer Corps withdrew into the city. The units of the Panzer Corps which were equipped with German weapons had urgent need of this ammunition. There was a small depot in the inner city, but it held mainly Russian 76mm ammunition, while the Germans had only four captured guns of this caliber. In addition, there was scarcely any ammunition available for those local defense forces equipped with captured weapons. Despite Propaganda Minister Goebbels's widely heralded air resupply of ammunition, rations, medical supplies and the like, from April 26–30 only eight rounds of ammunition for light field howitzers could be salvaged from the air drops.

Fuel was also short. Horse-drawn vehicles had to be employed to move ammunition and other supplies. The movement of motorized units was extremely adversely affected and required special permission. Even the movement of single vehicles required express permission.

Apart from local shortages, the provision of rations for the troops was generally satisfactory.

As with ammunition supplies, there were only a few large depots available, and they could not be evacuated completely when threatened by enemy attack. Although there were well-stocked food depots for the civilian population throughout the city, local shortages occurred during the course of the fighting. Generally, the food resupply seems to have been adequate despite the loss of the outer depots.

According to statistics, the population of Greater Berlin at the beginning of the war was about 4.3 million. After the collapse, the town had 2.5 million inhabitants. This reduction was due to the evacuation as a result of the bombings. Due to the speed of military developments, the bulk of the remaining civilian population in Berlin could not be evacuated. These civilians consisted of Berlin residents and refugees from eastern Germany. Their behavior during the fighting and the Soviet occupation was exemplary despite the burdens which exceeded all measure of tolerable standards.

The water supply could also maintained, despite extensive destruction of water works and mains, by use of wells, reservoirs, rivers and lakes.

The Luftwaffe and Air Resupply

Only minor elements of the Luftwaffe participated in the battles around Berlin.

Significant numbers of reserves (mostly sailors) and supplies aimed at increasing the combat-effectiveness of the defenders could not be flown in due to the early loss of the airfields of Gatow and Kladow. The sporadic air-dropping of supplies could in no way be viewed as meaningful reinforcement.

The difficulties associated with the use of the provisional runway constructed along the East-West Axis became clear when the renowned flier Hanna Reitsch managed to land there in her *Fieseler Storch* aircraft on April 26 with General Ritter von Greim (Göring's successor as Commander in Chief of the Luftwaffe) despite enemy artillery fire. Greim was wounded during this operation. The take-off on April 28 on the crater-riddled surface succeeded despite Soviet efforts to shoot down the plane with antiaircraft fire.

THE SOVIET OFFENSIVE FROM APRIL 16–21, 1945

Between April 12–15, 1945, the Soviets had carried out their preparatory attacks to extend their bridgehead at Küstrin, which necessitated the commitment of the Panzer Division *Müncheberg,* previously held in reserve. On the morning of April 16, a large-scale Soviet offensive began along the middle

Oder and the lower Neisse, supported by heavy artillery fire and air bombardment.

On the Oder front alone, the Soviets opened up a preparatory artillery barrage with 22,000 guns with an intensity hitherto unknown. They attacked with the First Belorussian Front. Marshal Zhukov's main thrust was delivered from the Küstrin bridgehead.

At the same time, supported by vastly superior artillery, the First Ukrainian Front attacked along the Neisse between Forst and Guben.

As early as April 16, while the Oder front was still between Frankfurt and Schwedt, Konev's troops broke through the position of the Fourth Panzer Army on the lower Neisse south of Guben. The divisions of the Ninth Army bore the brunt of the Soviet assault. Despite their inferior strength and materiel, they were able to hold in the Frankfurt sector and prevented the Soviets from crossing the Oder southeast of Eberswalde.

West of Küstrin, the Soviet assault troops accompanied by numerous tanks failed to capture the critically significant heights near Seelow on the western edge of the Oder valley on April 16–17. The Russian assaults did not succeed until the early hours of April 18.

Elements of General Weidling's reserve, LVIth Panzer Corps east of Berlin, had to be committed. During the battle, the 20th Panzer Division suffered heavy losses.

During the night of April 16–17, the Soviets achieved a deep penetration at the juncture of the XIth SS Corps and the LVIth Panzer Corps which was now in the front line. Communication with the XIth SS Corps was lost and could not be reestablished. Another penetration north of the LVIth Panzer Corps at the juncture with the C1 Corps led to a Soviet breakthrough from the area of Wriezen all the way to Tiefensee.

The German front west of Küstrin now began to crumble completely. Two days after the start of the offensive, the front on the northern wing of the Ninth Army also collapsed. Immediate counterattacks failed. The weak German forces had no chance against the enemy superiority. From the reserves in the Ninth Army's sector, the 25th Panzergrenadier Division had already entered the fighting on April 16.

By April 20, further reserves had to be committed to the battle: the 18th Panzergrenadier Division, the SS Panzergrenadier Division *Nordland,* and parts of the SS Panzergrenadier Division *Nederland.* The remaining elements of the LVIth Panzer Corps, which had hitherto remained in reserve, were also deployed. This corps included the 20th Panzer Division (almost destroyed), the Panzer Division *Müncheberg* (a newly created formation), the 9th Airborne Division (of low combat-value), the 18th Panzergrenadier Division (under command since April 17), SS Panzergrenadier Division *Nordland,* parts of SS Panzergrenadier Division *Nederland* and the 408th Peoples' Artillery Corps (six battalions, including two mortar battalions and two battalions of captured Russian 152mm guns).

The corps was not able to halt the Russians' offensive but was forced into a fighting withdrawal. It was only with difficulty that the 9th Airborne Division could be rallied.

Meanwhile, the deep penetration on the Neisse front in the Fourth Panzer Army sector had developed into a breakthrough. As the Vth Corps on the left wing of the Fourth Panzer Army could no longer be effectively controlled by the Army Group Center due to the enemy breakthrough, it was transferred on April 17 to Army Group Vistula for reasons of unified control and joined the Ninth Army.

Due to a lack of German reserves, the Fourth Panzer Army's broken front could not be restored. The weak reserves of the Fourth Panzer Army and the Ninth Army were urgently needed to protect their flanks. Hitler's orders—to close the breach through coordinated attacks by the Fourth Panzer Army from the south and by the Ninth Army holding on the Oder—could not be carried out.

The Second and Fourth Soviet Tank Armies rolled west and northwest with their numerous tanks and motorized forces almost unopposed. Hitler's view—that Dresden and Prague were the Soviet operational goals—was thus disproven.

It was the capital of the Reich that was directly threatened by this long-range outflanking movement of Konev's armies. At this point, the Army Group Vistula, still commanded by Berlin, ordered all available forces pulled out of the city. In view of the threat to the city from the south, the Division *Jahn* (a part of the Spree Group still being formed being out of young men of the Labor Service) was deployed on both sides of Baruth on a 40 kilometer wide front facing south.

The Russians, however, broke through this weak defensive line near Baruth as early as April 20. Enemy tank units reached the area around Jüterbog and Wünsdorf. The Ninth Army was surrounded to the south, on its flanks, and to the rear. The Soviets had broken through on the northern wing of the army. The Army Group Vistula's request to pull back the center and right wing of the Ninth Army was denied. As a result of this decision, in a few days the army was completely encircled.

In the meantime, efforts were made to halt the enemy advance east of Berlin on the Fürstenwalde-Straussberg-Bernau line. The LVIth Panzer Corps tried to stop the thrust of strong Soviet armored forces west of Buckow in the Märkischen Schweiz with a counterattack by the 18th Panzergrenadier Division and the SS Panzergrenadier Division *Nordland,* but this attempt failed after initial success due to superior enemy firepower.

To protect the deep right flank of the Third Panzer Army, which had not yet been frontally attacked and which was threatened by the enemy advance via Bernau toward the west, security detachments of the Army Group Vistula had been posted on the Hohenzollern Canal, at Oranienburg and on the Finow Canal. From Oranienburg up to Eberswalde, they were assigned to SS *Obergruppenführer* [Lieutenant General] Steiner. These forces consisted entirely of a mixture of units which had been thrown together including *Alarmeinheiten, Volkssturm,* units cut off from the Ninth Army, and improvised units mostly consisting of Luftwaffe personnel. The only units of what became known as the "Steiner Group" that could be called combat-effective were the 25th Panzergrenadier Division and the 7th Panzer Division which joined it later.

When the Army Group Vistula attempted to establish a defensive front against the danger of a southern encirclement of the Third Panzer Army, the Second Belorussian Front under Marshal Rokossovsky, which had halted on the lower Oder, attacked on April 21. During the first few days the Third Panzer Army was able to hold its positions between Schwedt and Stettin.

On the same day, however, it became clear that all German defensive positions along the outer limits of Berlin had been pierced. In the first few days of the offensive, the troops of General Perchorowitsch and the armored units of General Bogdanov had outflanked Berlin from the north. From the east of the forces of Generals Kusnezov, Bersarin and Chuikov were attacking.

An analysis of the situation revealed that the main assault axis was aimed at Berlin. The thrust over the Neisse into the region of Saxony and the attacks south of Stettin were merely aimed at tying down strong German forces with the objective to gain as much territory as possible and more deep penetrations to the west.

THE GERMAN HIGH COMMAND AND THE ARMY GROUP VISTULA BEFORE AND DURING THE OPERATIONS WHICH LED TO THE ENCIRCLEMENT OF BERLIN

The Army Group Vistula had tried in vain to spare Berlin the cruel and hopeless struggle. The plan of the Army Group in case of Soviet breakthrough was to conduct a fighting withdrawal to the northwest. According to this plan, the Ninth Army was to pull back in northwesterly direction on both sides of the capital. The difficulties of such an operation were fully realized, particularly as it was expected (and later proven by events) that the main thrust of the Soviet advance would be aimed at the left wing of the Ninth Army. The majority of the reserves were, therefore, concentrated here so that while holding the left wing, the right wing and center could conduct

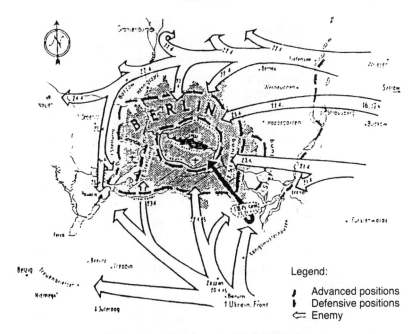

The Soviet Offensive, April 16–25, 1945.

a fighting withdrawal to the northwest. Under this plan the integrity of the Army Group would be maintained intact. The evacuation of defensive forces from Berlin during the short time that the city was under the Army Group's direct control was also aimed at stripping the local defensive positions to save the populace from the prospect of senseless bloody combat.

However, the bulk of the defensive forces had to stay in Berlin. The lack of transport, equipment and combat strength of most units, so essential to the successful conduct of mobile operations, did not permit their use outside the city. A reorganization into combat units was not possible due to lack of time and materiel.

In addition, Hitler intervened once again.

It is true that in his dramatic situation conference in the Reich Chancellery on April 22, he had decided to stay in Berlin and to take personal control of the fighting while ordering Generals Keitel and Jodl and *Reichsleiter* Bormann to fly to southern Germany to continue directing the war from there. However, all three refused to carry out the order.

Hitler allowed himself to be swayed. He accepted General Jodl's suggestion to turn around those German units on the western front facing the Western Allies, to throw them into the fight for Berlin and to have the OKW control this operation.

For this purpose, the OKW and the Wehrmacht Operations Staff were combined into a single OKW Staff on April 22. On April 25 the Army General Staff was also incorporated into this unified staff.

General Krebs, who had taken over for General Guderian as Acting Chief of the Army General Staff on April 29, 1945, remained Hitler's principal military advisor with him in the Reich Chancellery. Bormann also shared his fate.

Keitel and Jodl, however, took on the task of controlling the relief operations around the capital of the Reich.

In the meantime, Hitler—bypassing the Army Group Vistula and the Ninth Army—ordered the LVIth Panzer Corps to reinforce the Berlin defenses.

The Ninth Army had received explicit orders [from the Army Group Vistula] to hold its position. Hitler's new order not only frustrated the plans of the Army Group to preserve the Ninth Army, but he and his High Command rendered the entire conception of the Army Group illusory. Hitler ordered counterattacks to relieve the now almost completely encircled capital of the Reich. The forces to be used were the Ninth Army from the south, the Twelfth Army from the west and the Steiner Group from the north.

The Ninth Army faced an impossible task. With its weak forces, it was engaged in a desperate struggle with a vastly superior enemy. It was not able to gain for itself the operational freedom so essential for such a difficult task as was posed by the relief of the encircled capital of the Reich to its rear. The Twelfth Army was also confronted right from the start of its operations with a dual task. On the one hand, it was to fight in the west to prevent an American advance across the

Elbe and Mulde in the area of Magdeburg to as far south as Dessau. On the other hand, the instructions of April 20 from the Wehrmacht Operations Staff specified pulling back the left wing of the Twelfth Army to the Jüterbog-Torgau line in the event of further Soviet advances toward the Elbe. For this purpose a strong reserve was to be formed behind the left wing in the Jüterbog area. The Twelfth Army remained for the time being under direct control of the combined OKW-Wehrmacht Operations Staff.

Both the relief attack from the north and the use of the Ninth Army for relief operations contradicted the plans of the Army Group Vistula.

According to their perception, the priorities were not only to protect the badly demolished southern flank of the Third Panzer Army, ripped open a deep Soviet penetration over the Oder, but also to protect the rear of the Army Group from the threat of an enemy advance developing across the Havel.

THE FIGHTING AND RELIEF ATTEMPTS FROM APRIL 22–MAY 2, 1945

The Development of the Situation around Berlin from April 22–April 25

As early as April 22, the forces attacking via Zossen were on the southern edge of Berlin. Parts of the Division *Jahn* were falling back on Potsdam. East of the city, the enemy had advanced to Erkner and Hoppegarten. The LVIth Panzer Corps, executing a delaying action, had to be withdrawn to the Köpenick-Bliesdorf line as the enemy had already penetrated the outer periphery of Berlin with an outflanking movement north of Hoppegarten. On April 22 they broke into the suburbs of Weissensee and Pankow. Encirclement was also threatening in the south. Communications with the Ninth Army were lost.

The disengagement of the Panzer Corps, ordered for the night of April 21–22 and involving four motorized divisions and a Peoples' Artillery Corps, had to be conducted along a single road. It was only thanks to the energetic efforts of the military traffic control authorities, who had orders to prevent passing and to maintain discipline (by force of arms if needed) that the columns were successfully moved. The man in charge of this operation, Colonel Wöhlermann, Artillery Commander of the LVIth Panzer Corps, reported as follows: "At the major congestion point, in complete darkness and with the use of a flashlight and pistol, I enforced my authority as a Colonel and Artillery Commander of the Corps in a laborious struggle lasting several hours which gradually got the convoys of four and five abreast moving again in a steady flow."

In the north, the advanced elements of the Russian forces pushing westwards from Werneuchen via Bernau had already reached the Havel sector between Spandau and Oranienburg on April 22.

The Brigade Müller, sent to occupy this sector from Döberitz, consisted of a few weak battalions. It was not possible to establish whether they were able to take up position in time or not. In any case, Soviet tanks crossed the Havel at Henningsdorf north of Spandau that same day. In so doing, they destroyed the weak German security forces in their path. It was their aim to encircle Berlin from the west. At Oranienburg, an enemy attempt to cross the Oder-Havel Canal was frustrated by the two leading battalions of a naval division which was just arriving.

The Berlin Defense Zone was removed from the Army Group Vistula's command after only four short days. Berlin was placed under Hitler's direct command.

In the meantime, the decision was made to employ the Twelfth Army (Army Wenck) in the relief attempt on Berlin. It was to concentrate strong forces for a thrust northwest toward Berlin and later, by attacking toward Potsdam, to link up with the Ninth Army.

This, however, revealed a problem: the need to secure the staging area against the Soviets who were advancing on a broad front toward the Wittenberg(Elbe)-Brandenburg(Havel) line.

On the old front, facing west, only weak security detachments remained. This was done on the assumption that the Americans would remain in their present position, as had already happened. The bulk of the Twelfth Army was now assembled for a thrust against the eastern enemy. Security and reconnaissance forces were immediately directed against the assumed locations of Soviet units.

The protection of the Army's flanks became especially important. General Wenck was concerned about anchoring his southern flank against enemy pressure between Wittenberg and Niemegk and securing his northern flank southeast of Brandenburg (Havel).

He received the following order from OKW on April 23 at 0305 hours:

> The enemy has reached Drewitz and Grossbeeren with tank and reconnaissance forces. We expect strong enemy assaults at Potsdam. Parts of the Division *Jahn* are being employed against the enemy, advancing on both sides of the Treuenbrietzen-Beelitz road. The Twelfth Army will leave weak securing forces on the Elbe and on April 24 will attack the enemy in the Jütebog-Treuenbrietzen area from the west, and will establish contact with the Potsdam Combat Commandant on the autobahn three kilometers south of Ferch. The Potsdam Combat Commandant, under direct command of the command of the Army General Staff, will defend the Havel lakes in the section of the autobahn triangle Caputh-Potsdam, its front facing east to screen the Krampnitz lake toward the south. For this purpose it will be assigned the guard company of the Chief of the Army General Staff. The Havel bridges between Potsdam and Glienicke are to be demolished.

The aim was to relieve Berlin by means of the Twelfth Army attacking to the east into the left flank of the Third Soviet Tank Army. This was supposed to demonstrate to the Americans that the first priority was the fight against the Soviets.

The Ninth Army was to reverse its front and join up with the Twelfth Army. Although the Twelfth Army had not yet completed its organization, its young soldiers had shown excellent fighting spirit in combat with the Americans. The XXth Corps, consisting of three divisions commanded by General Köhler, was the strongest formation in the Twelfth Army. In the meantime, the Berlin Defense Zone had been subjected to further heavy Soviet attacks. Their main attacks were in the southeast, at the Teltow Canal. They pushed into the outer city defense ring in the south, east and north.

In the south they reached Zehlendorf; in the east they reached the inner defense ring and were only halted in the area of the Friedrichshain antiaircraft tower, while in the north they achieved a deep penetration in the Tegel area. Simultaneously, the Soviets pushed on toward Döberitz, exploiting their successful Havel crossings of the previous day. Other formations further south finally had closed the circle around Berlin from the west on the evening of April 24. Potsdam was encircled next.

Zhukov's and Konev's leading tank units joined up south of Nauen.

Army Group Vistula's fears of a Russian thrust deep in the southern flank of the Third Panzer Army and in the rear of the Army Group were confirmed when considerable Soviet advance forces broke through to Döberitz on April 23 and to the Rathenow area on April 25.

It was possible to throw up a weak defensive barrier connecting to our forces northwest of Oranienburg by bringing in the XLIst Panzer Corps (General Holste), detached from the Twelfth Army on the Elbe front, and parts of Steiner's forces to oppose the Russians. General von Tippelskirch and the staff of the Twenty-first Army assumed command of the sector from the lower Havel to the area south of Neuruppin.

North of Berlin, General Steiner of the Army Group Vistula received orders on April 23 to mount a relief offensive to the south. He had about seven battalions of varying combat-effectiveness for this operation. The attack began early on April 24. It pushed forward against a weak and surprised enemy to the Zehlendorf line and to Klosterfelde, about 10 kilometers south of the Finow Canal. Then superior enemy pressure forced the German formations back to their starting positions.

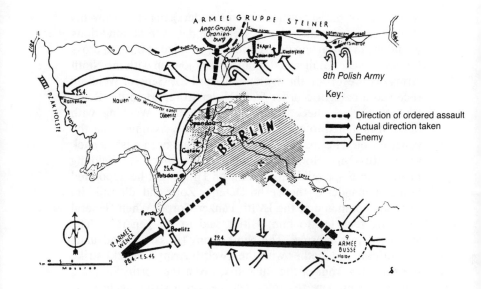

German relief attacks assaults April–May 1, 1945.

In a manner similar to Steiner's attack, enemy forces were tied down in the Eberswalde area. For days the Eighth Polish Army attacked the German bridgehead there without being able to eliminate it.

The Transfer of the LVIth Panzer Corps into Berlin and the Battles in the City

The story of the transfer of the LVIth Panzer Corps into Berlin is evidence of the turbulent command conditions of those days and deserves to be recorded.

After the LVIth Panzer Corps had already been involved in severe fighting east of Berlin, the corps commander informed his divisional and regimental commanders that he had been ordered by the command of the Ninth Army to make contact with them, but had also been ordered by Hitler to take his corps to Berlin. As it was clear to the corps commander (as it

was to all of his subordinate commanders) that to throw his
Panzer corps into the ruins of Berlin under current conditions
would mean its certain destruction, he decided at once to cross
the Spree near Königswusterhausen and join up with the Ninth
Army. However, on the evening of April 23, General Weidling
received a categoric order from Hitler to report to the Reich
Chancellery at once. This order threatened Weidling with
death if he failed to obey. It was commonly assumed that the
general would be shot because his corps had been pushed back
by the Russians. However, events proved otherwise. Weidling
made such a splendid impression on Hitler that he appointed
him Commander of the Berlin Defense Zone and allowed him
to retain command of the LVIth Panzer Corps. When General
Weidling reported to him, Hitler said to the general, "The
situation must improve. The Ninth Army (Busse) will advance
on Berlin and, together with the Twelfth Army (Wenck) strike
the southern front of the Russians. From the north, Steiner's
troops will prepare to attack and deliver a strike against the
northern wing."

Following his appointment as Commander of the Berlin
Defense Zone, General Weidling moved the LVIth Panzer
Corps into Berlin during April 23–24.

The local garrisons, who could scarcely defend themselves
against enemy attacks, now were reinforced by combat-hard-
ened units. The situation east of the city had become particularly threatening.

General Weidling gave immediate instructions that each pair
of the eight existing Berlin Defense Sectors should be placed
under the command of one of the four divisional commanders
of the Panzer Corps. The sectors were designed from the
northeast in a clockwise direction from Sector A to Sector H.
Sector D, for example, ran from Zehlendorf (inclusive) to
Neuköln (inclusive). This measure was probably adopted primarily to make use of the existing command structure and
secondarily to ensure that combat-proven experienced commanders became decisively involved in conducting the defense. These measures of the corps commander and new
commander of the Berlin Defense Zone, although correct in

principle under the existing conditions, also caused some friction when two strong personalities clashed with each other. This occurred in Sector A, commanded by the aggressive Lieutenant Colonel Bärenfänger. Serious differences arose between him and the new sector commander Brigadier General Mummert, Commander of Panzer Division *Müncheberg*.

The formations of the LVIth Panzer Corps were deployed according to the degree of the threat and the importance of the defense sector as follows: 20th Panzer Division with its remnants around Wannsee in the southwest of the city; Panzer Division *Müncheberg* in the south and southeast (it still had 15–20 tanks); Panzergrenadier Division *Nordland*, consisting of Scandinavian volunteers and a French SS *Sturmbataillon Charlemagne* and remnants of the Panzergrenadier Division *Nederland* in the eastern sector; 18th Panzergrenadier Division north and south of the "Zoo" sector.

The remnants of other frontline formations, i.e. those of the Ninth Airborne Division, were divided.

The strengths and combat-effectiveness of these formations varied. The Division *Müncheberg* and the 18th Panzergrenadier Division could be considered to have about half their original combat strength and were capable of fighting, even though somewhat reduced. The Division *Nordland* was slightly weaker in combat-effectiveness but could also be considered capable of fighting.

The 20th Panzer Division and the remnants of the Division *Nederland* were so badly battered that they had little combat value; the same applied to the remnants of other units.

The 408th Peoples' Artillery Corps, which was attached to the LVIth Panzer Corps, had been able to bring two-thirds of its guns to Berlin, although it had practically no more ammunition.

In total, the artillery in the Berlin Defense Zone consisted of the weak stationary artillery with foreign pieces, the 408th Peoples' Artillery Corps, and the regular artillery of the divisions of the LVIth Panzer Corps.

The problem was to find positions for the artillery brought into Berlin. The only suitable sites in the center of the extensively damaged city were: the zoo, certain larger squares such as Lützowplatz, Belle Alliance Platz, Lustgarten, Alexanderplatz, etc., and the railway yards at the Potsdam and Anhalt train stations.

The Defense Zone Artillery Commander—now provided by the LVIth Panzer Corps—worked closely together with the 1st Antiaircraft Artillery Division. Both combat headquarters were in the *Flakleitstand* "Zoo." In conjunction with the heavy twin antiaircraft guns of the antiaircraft bunker, the defensive artillery fire concentration zones were formed.

Apart from the 60,000 or so *Volkssturm* members within the encircled city of Berlin, the army units had at most the equivalent personnel strength of 4–5 divisions and at most 40–50 tanks. With the exception of the few intact units—especially the LVIth Panzer Corps and the SS Brigade Mohnke—they were not organically integrated units, but as already explained, a hodgepodge of remnants and splinter groups thrown together without formal organization. With varying quality and degrees of training, armament and equipment, their combat value was accordingly low.

The Attacks to Relieve Berlin, April 24–28

While the fighting in Berlin became more and more bitter, the XXth Army Corps (Köhler) of the Twelfth Army in the Niemegk area was preparing an assault in the direction of Trebbin.

On the evening of April 24, the Twelfth Army received an OKW order to launch a relief attack on Berlin. Due to the advance of Marshal Konev's troops south of Berlin, the Twelfth Army was forced from April 25 on to prevent any further progress through flexible combat operations. It proved impossible to form a contiguous front line in the Twelfth Army's extensive area of operation. In a series of individual operations, the enemy suffered considerable losses.

The weak XLIst Panzer Corps (General Holste), on the northern wing of the army, was to attack Nauen. Due to special difficulties in providing mobility for this formation, there was little prospect of success.

The three divisions of the XXth Corps now ready to attack were up to strength so far as personnel were concerned, but were insufficiently motorized, had too few assault guns, were poorly armed, and had inadequate command structures. Despite these inadequacies, however, General Wenck considered the combat spirit of these troops splendid; their leadership was especially good.

As early as April 23, General Busse had sought to save his Ninth Army from destruction by extracting it from the threat of being enriched southeast of Berlin, even though General Krebs, Chief of the Army General Staff in the Reich Chancellery, was unwilling to give permission to withdraw to the west. Finally, after much back and forth and the involvement of the Commander in Chief of the Army Group Vistula (General Heinrici), it was possible to get a decision from Hitler which read, "The Führer agrees to the withdrawal of the most northeastern elements of the Ninth Army to a defined line." This general formulation was translated by the Army Group Vistula into the following order: "Break through to the west. Right shoulder on the Südring autobahn to link up with Wenck. Contact on the eastern front no longer required."

While the orders to the Twelfth and Ninth Armies expressed the hopes for a union of both armies and a joint relief of Berlin, that same day the Soviets and Americans linked up at Torgau on the Elbe. The Soviets reported this event: "The troops of the First Ukrainian Front and the Allied Anglo-American Troops have split the German fronts from the east and west and have made contact with one another on April 25 at 1330 hours in the center of Germany, at the town of Torgau. The German troops in the southern areas of Germany are thus cut off . . ."

On this day, Hitler expressed a particular interest in the accelerated intervention of Steiner's Group from the north in the battle for Berlin. For this purpose Steiner was to attack out of the area northwest of Oranienburg with the 25th Panzergrenadier Division (with the task force of the 7th Panzer Division under command) against the deep flank of the Russians advancing toward the west at Nauen.

Meanwhile, however, in a large-scale offensive south of Stettin on April 25, the Russians had broken through the front of the Third Panzer Army. In a telex to General Jodl (OKW) and the Twelfth Army which arrived at OKW at 0025 hours on April 26, Hitler ordered that the expansion of the already extensive Soviet bridgehead be prevented. On this day—April 26, 1945—Hitler ordered the Ninth and Twelfth Armies to turn north after joining up to destroy the enemy in the south of Berlin and to establish communications with the capital of the Reich.

Hitler still insisted on a relief attack from the north.

The request of the Commander in Chief of the Army Group Vistula to cancel the attack was refused, even though the Russian bridgehead south of Stettin had already achieved operational significance. The command of the emergency reserves in the Fürstenberg-Neustrelitz-Neubrandenburg line was assumed by the Twenty-first Army High Command under General von Tippelskirch.

German chances for an offensive victory dwindled after attacks by superior enemy forces on April 26 against the bridgehead formed by the 25th Panzergrenadier Division south of the Ruppin Canal. With the "Führer Order" of April 27, Hitler ordered that the Assault Group Oranienburg (the reinforced 25th Panzergrenadier Division) be placed under the command of General Holste's XLIst Panzer Corps. General Steiner was to be removed. On April 27 the situation took another unfavorable turn against the Germans.

At 1500 hours, it became clear that the enemy had broken through the Third Panzer Army at Prenzlau. There were no more reserves available. The reinforced 25th Panzergrenadier Division had to be relieved of its current assault task in order to mount a thrust into the southern flank of the enemy breakthrough thrust. But the OKW still clung to the hope that it would be able to proceed with the attack at Oranienburg later. OKW ordered the bridgehead there to be held.

On April 27 the Twelfth Army and the Infantry Division *Schlageter* were placed under the command of Army Group Vistula.

In a telephone conversation at 0300 hours on April 28 between Field Marshal Keitel and Chief of the Army General Staff General Krebs who was with Hitler in the Reich Chancellery, Keitel informed Krebs of the increasingly likely failure of the attack from the north. Krebs finally stated that Hitler could only hold out in the Reich Chancellery for a maximum of 48 hours. If no help had arrived by then, it would be too late. Telephone communications with the Reich Chancellery ended at 0500 hours. Nothing characterized the development of the situation up to April 28 better than this call for help from the Reich Chancellery.

The Deterioration of the Situation in Berlin and the Fighting in the City Center

On April 24, 1945, the actual battle for Berlin began following heavy artillery preparation and aerial bombardment. In the following days, this led to a steadily deteriorating situation. The troops of the Red Army, attacking in every city sector, drove the defenders back to the circular railway.

The enemy pushed forward from house to house, street to street, following artillery preparation and supported by tanks, heavy weapons, flame throwers and army engineers. Experienced in all aspects of urban combat, they avoided and by-passed the stronger pockets of German resistance. With their strong infantry and ample reserves, they cracked open the German positions. The German defenders were exhausted from their continuous defense; their combat strength dropped day by day, and many were those for whom the constant physical and psychological pressure became too much to bear.

Two eye-witness accounts may serve to demonstrate the scale and bitterness of the battle. An aide-de-camp of the Division *Müncheberg,* which was under General Mummert's command, reported:*

---

*Partial quotation excerpted from Jürgen Thorwald, *Die grosse Flucht.* Munich, 1979.

April 25, 0530 hours: Attack by new massed tank forces. Forced to withdraw. Orders from the Reich Chancellery: Division *Müncheberg* is to move at once to Alexanderplatz for a relief attack.

0900 hours: order cancelled while we are moving out. By 1000 hours the Russians are pushing relentlessly forward toward Tempelhof airfield. New main defense line is Rathaus Schöneberg-Hallesches Tor-Belle Alliance Platz. Heavy street fighting. Many dead civilians. Dying animals. Women flee from cellar to cellar. . . . New orders: to Alexanderplatz. . . .

April 26: the night red with fire. Heavy artillery fire. . . . At about 0530 hours, renewed intensive artillery barrage. . . . Retreat to the Anhalt Station. . . .

New combat headquarters at Anhalt Station. Platforms and waiting rooms resemble an army camp. . . . Exploding shells shake the tunnel roofs. Chucks of concrete collapse. Smell of powder and clouds of smoke in the tunnels. Hospital trains of the underground municipal railway roll along slowly. Suddenly a surprise. Water pours into our combat headquarters. Screams, weeping, cursing, people fight for the ladders which lead to the surface through the ventilation shafts. The masses pour over the railway sleepers leaving children and wounded behind. . . . The water rises over a meter before it slowly recedes. The terrible fear and panic lasts for more than an hour. Many drowned. The cause: on somebody's orders engineers had demolished the sides of the Landwehr Canal between the Schöneberg and Möckern bridges in order to flood the tunnels to block underground enemy advances. . . . Late afternoon, we move to Potsdam Platz. Combat headquarters in the second floor as the tunnels are still deep under water. Shells penetrate the roof. Heavy losses above, civilians and wounded. Smoke pours through the shell holes. . . . After one heavy shell explosion under the first level landing of the stairs by the station entrance next to the Pschorr brewery, there is a horrible sight: men, soldiers, women and children are literally plastered to the walls. . . .

April 27: Attacks continued all night. Russians try to break through to Leipziger Strasse. Prinz Albrecht Strasse is recaptured. . . . Increasing signs of dissolution. . . . But we cannot capitulate at the last moment and then regret for the rest of our lives that we did not hold out. Physical conditions are

indescribable. Neither relief nor rest. No regular food. Scarcely
any bread. Nervous breakdowns under the continuous artillery
fire. Water is pumped out of the tunnels and from the Spree and
filtered. . . .

Flying courts-martial appear among us, especially frequent
today. Most are very young SS *Führer*. Hardly any decorations.
They are blind and fanatical. Hopes of relief and the simultaneous fear of the courts-martial revitalize the men again. General
Mummert bans the reappearance of any flying courts-martial in
this defense sector. A division with the most bearers of the
Knight's Cross and the oak leaf cluster does not deserve to be
persecuted by such young fellows. Mummert is determined
personally to shoot one such court-martial that interfered in his
sector.

Potsdamer Platz is a wasteland. There are countless damaged
vehicles. The wounded are still lying in the shot-up ambulances.
Dead everywhere. Mostly run over by tanks and hideously
disfigured.

In the evening, an attempt to break through to the Ministry of
Propaganda to get some news about Wenck from inside one of
the government buildings. Rumors that the Ninth Army is on its
way to Berlin. In the West, a general armistice is being concluded. At nightfall, the heaviest fire in the city center. At the
same time, there are attacks on our position. We can no longer
hold Potsdamer Platz, so we move out underground at about
0400 hours to Nollendorf Platz. In the opposite tunnel, the
Russians move toward Potsdamer Platz.

Thus the defenders of Berlin fought on desperately in the
hope that they would still be relieved.

Another eye-witness, the Artillery Commander of the LVIth
Panzer Corps, Colonel Wöhlermann, described the situation:

Main centers of the defense were Friedrichshain, Alexanderplatz
with the Police Presidium, the Ministry of Aviation and Leipziger
Platz. While the "Birkbuschriegel" held in Steglitz, the Russians
were in "Unter den Eichen" in Zehlendorf and at "Wilden
Eber" in Dahlem. The Stössensee bridge, the area around the
radio tower and the road via Ruhleben to Spandau remained
open until the last days in April. The Soviets pushed through to

Charlottenburg via the Jungfernheide station and Gartenfeld. In
a rapid advance they took the Salzufer across the Technical
University. Greatly superior forces advanced through the small
300 and past the Criminal Court to the Spree River and, against
bitter defense, crossed the remains of the incompletely demolished Moltke Bridge to take possession of the ruins of the
Reichstag.

The Soviets reported: "On April 30 Sergeants Kantarya and
Yegorov, soldiers of Captain Neustroyev's battalion, hoisted
the victory banner of the Red Army on the Reichstag building."

The Cornelius Bridge and the Savarin area are also hotly
contested, as were the corners of Budapester Strasse and
Nürnberger Strasse, the Eden Hotel and the old army clothing
store. Some Soviet tanks, which had fought their way into the
Zoological Garden, fired at the steel window shutters of the
antiaircraft towers there. The platforms of the antiaircraft
towers and the immediate vicinity from now on were con-
stantly under fire.

Colonel Wöhlermann reported, "From the platform of the
antiaircraft tower with its great height, one had a panoramic
view of the burning, smoldering and smoking great city, a
scene which again and again shook one to the core."

The Defense Sector "Citadel" had been established around
the Reich Chancellery which housed Hitler and his entourage.
This sector was commanded by General Mohnke, who was in
charge of some 1,000 soldiers including Balts, many French,
Belgians, Flemish, Dutch, Scandinavians, Swiss, British and
Spaniards. All had volunteered to serve in the SS. They fought
bitterly against the Soviet assault on the city center. The SS
Sturmbataillon Charlemagne destroyed more than 60 tanks in
eight days. It suffered heavy losses. Of the 300 soldiers transferred into the city on April 24, only 30 were still alive on May
2 after they had fought to the end.

In all this chaos, the inhabitants of Berlin were exposed to
the horrors of war, and the women in particular fell prey to the
greed of the victors. At the same time that encouraging slogans

were being broadcast, execution commandos, mostly formed of party officials, sought to eradicate any and every trace of "defeatism" and "treachery" with death and the threat of death in blind obedience to Goebbels's propaganda.

The Failure of the Relief Attacks on Berlin

In southwest Berlin on April 28, the Twelfth Army had achieved a limited offensive success with the XXth Corps. They had managed to advance to the Beelitz-Ferch-Petzow line. Contact was made with General Reymann's garrison in Potsdam. They evaded Russian clutches by withdrawing on the waterways and made contact with the Twelfth Army at Ferch on the southwestern tip of Lake Schwielov. Here they were picked up.

In the early hours of April 28, news arrived from the encircled Ninth Army in the area of Halbe that their breakout attempt had failed. The Ninth Army was trapped in a pocket in Märkisch Buchholz. They were penned up together with the civilian population and in a desperate situation. Air resupply for the army failed, and radio communications terminated on April 29. The higher command echelons did not know where the army was or what had happened to it, even though the distance to Beelitz—where they were supposed to join up with the Twelfth Army (Wenck)—was only about 70 kilometers.

On April 28 and 29, the Twelfth Army had to fend off numerous heavy enemy attacks which made a relief attempt on Berlin impossible. The OKW was forced to accept this. Holste's corps could not carry out its mission—to come to Berlin's aid—for the same reason.

In the meantime, General Heinrici, aware of his responsibilities as Commander in Chief of the Army Group Vistula and recognizing the increasingly untenable situation of his units, had withdrawn his right wing back over the Havel-Voss Canal line of the Havel river to avoid sacrificing his forces. An attack on Berlin from the north had become senseless and impossible. General Heinrici was removed from command because some officials still cling to the fiction that Berlin could be liberated by his armies, although that was utterly impossible. In this situation of imminent and unavoidable defeat, he refused to waste more human lives. By early morning on May 1, the remnants of the Ninth Army had managed to fight their way out of their encirclement with heavy losses and join up with the Twelfth Army at Beelitz. General Busse's army was unable to continue fighting. In the forests of Märkisch Buchholz, Halbe and Teupitz, tens of thousands of soldiers and refugees were left behind. Only a few survived. This would not have happened had the General been allowed to withdraw in time. The military cemetery in Halbe today holds about 20,000 mostly unknown soldiers.

In answer to Hitler's desperate call for relief, the OKW confirmed by radio early April 30, 1945 that there was no prospect of Berlin being relieved.

The Twelfth Army and as few as 30,000 of the Ninth Army, who had been able to break through to the Twelfth, managed to break out to the west. They surrendered to the Americans while the majority of the Army Group Vistula fell back to the British-American lines.

The Final Struggle and the Capitulation of Berlin

The fighting in the city was also nearing its end. The remnants of the defenders were concentrated in the so-called "Fortress Citadel" near the Reich Chancellery, the "Fortress Bendlerblock" and "Fortress Zoo Bunker." From the Zoo, a narrow corridor led to the west. The Reich Sport Field, the Spree River and the west bank of the Havel between Spandau and Wannsee were still being held. Orders and counter-orders to break out of Berlin or to stand and fight heightened the tension and caused great confusion.

At the same time, the news of Hitler's death—he had committed suicide on April 30—had become known.

On April 30, at 1345 hours, General Weidling had received a memo bearing Hitler's signature, dated "Reich Chancellery, April 30, 1945, 1330 hours." In this memo, Hitler permitted the defenders to break out of Berlin but forbade capitulation.

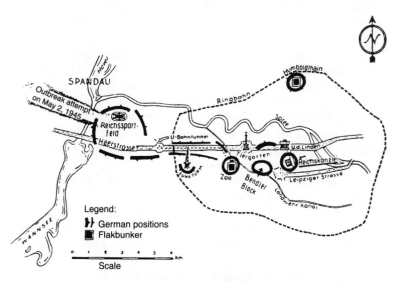

The situation on May 1, 1945 in Berlin.

When Weidling gave permission for independent breakout attempts, Goebbels (appointed Reich Chancellor in Hitler's Testament), forbade the breakout and simultaneously announced that he wanted to negotiate with the Russians. Weidling withdrew his permission.

Goebbels's capitulation negotiations, carried out by General Krebs with General Chuikov, failed. Shortly thereafter, Goebbels committed suicide.

Another capitulation offer, made by State Secretary Hans Fritzsche without knowledge of Goebbels's offer, was turned down by the Soviets.

General Weidling now stepped in and decided to capitulate. The Russians demanded an unconditional surrender. Continuing the fighting had become meaningless. The capitulation became effective on May 2, 1945.

The Information Bureau of the Soviet Union reports it thus:

"The garrison defending Berlin, led by the commander of the Berlin defense General Weidling and his staff, ceased their defense at 1500 hours on May 2, laid down their arms, and surrendered."

The capitulation was adhered to by Weidling's troops in the city center. But in other city districts, units had only received Weidling's breakout order and not the cancellation, or had received no orders at all. They had as little desire to surrender as the SS who were defending the government quarter.

The fighting went on for days. In the hectic, doom-ridden madness which had seized the city, those soldiers who had capitulated were labelled "traitors."

In Halensee and in various other places, the fighting went on literally to the last man.

Breakout attempts by small groups and individuals were sometimes successful. Stronger forces which tried to break out at Pankow were crushed by fire and in hand to hand combat.

A mass breakout through Spandau toward Nauen by the Division *Müncheberg* and parts of the 18th Panzergrenadier Division (to whom many civilians had attached themselves) succeeded in getting as far as Staaken despite incredibly heavy losses. From there, only small groups or individuals were able to fight their way further westward. Most were killed or fell into enemy hands.

The Battle for Berlin ended in misery and ruins, and death and captivity.

PART THREE

Reflections on the Events of 1945

In 1980, Joachim Schultz-Naumann, recorder of the War Diary of the High Command of the Armed Forces, and Wolfgang Paul, author of a World War II trilogy, recreated in this interview the final phase of the war, both as it was and as it is seen today. Schultz-Naumann has attempted to relate the events of 1945 based on his personel memories and brief notes.

Paul: You were one of the few officers from the front who were taken into the Wehrmacht command staff in the last weeks of the war. You survived the flight from West Prussia after amputation of a leg, served as Operations Officer of the Fortress of Deutsch-Krone and then went to Zossen in the Wehrmacht Operations Staff at Camp Zeppelin. Did you enter Camp Zeppelin at the beginning of March 1945 with a fatalistic attitude, or did you believe that important decisions could still emanate from their highest command echelon?

Schultz-Naumann: I did not enter this camp in a fatalistic mood; I went there quite soberly. I had set myself the goal of doing my job as well as possible. That is what I had done throughout the war. Of course, I knew what a difficult situation we were in and that the war would probably end badly for Germany in the next few weeks, I did not go there under the impression that great plans or decisions could be made. Circumstances did not allow this.

185

Paul: What was it like in Camp Zeppelin, and how did the work get done? As far as I know, the documents for the situation briefing for Hitler had to be prepared there.

Schultz-Naumann: Camp Zeppelin, located near Zossen, was extensive. It was divided into security zones, one for the High Command of the Armed Forces (OKW) and one for the Wehrmacht Operations Staff (WFSt), one for the Army High Command (OKH) and others. One could only enter with a special pass and numerous checks. In the Operations Section Army West, to which I belonged, the mornings were especially busy as the reports from the front had to be evaluated and transferred into the operations map. They had to be ready by 1500 hours for Hitler's afternoon situation conference. Prior to this, the Wehrmacht Report had to be completed by Wilhelm Ritter von Schramm. General Jodl, Chief of the Wehrmacht Operations Staff, had to give permission for its release.

We worked under enormous pressure. Prior to the situation conference with Hitler, where the chiefs of the operations sections of the Army, Air Force, and Navy, and sometimes department chiefs had to be present, there was a daily general situation conference at 1100 hours chaired by Deputy Chief of Wehrmacht Operations General Winter.

Staff work was obstructed by ponderous and inappropriate organization. Hitler was in the Reich Chancellery, mostly in the bunker. Jodl and Keitel lived in separate villas in Dahlem, each with a small staff. The working staffs of the OKW and WFSt were in Camp Zeppelin. The chain of command for decisions, e.g. for the western front, went from the Operations Section in charge, Army West (Major Friedel) to the Chief of Army Operations Section, (Colonel Meyer-Detring), then to the Deputy Chief of Operations of the Armed Forces High Command (General Winter). From Winter to the Chief of Operations of the Armed Forces High Command (General Jodl) and finally to the Supreme Commander of the Armed Forces, (Hitler). To speed up this process, the Chief of the Army Operations Section mostly excluded himself and allowed Major Friedel to report directly to the Chief of Operations of the Armed Forces High Command. The chain of command, owing also to its physical dispersion, precluded speedy decision-making.

The main cause of the delay was in fact that Hitler himself hardly ever made timely decisions. He often criticized proposals, lost himself in details, did not listen to reasonable advice, and sometimes had absurd ideas which were repeatedly proven impractical. Hitler often simply ignored proposals: probably the Supreme Commander of the Armed Forces either could not make up his mind, or the proposals did not please him. However, as the situation usually demanded a rapid decision, the military commanders often took independent action, or the problem was relegated to the next situation conference, i.e. the so-called "Night Briefing." Precious time was lost and decisions were frequently made too late because the situation—as is usual in war—had already changed. There was no decisive leadership. When operations failed, he did not see that he was at fault but sought scapegoats. This caused the high replacement rate of military commanders that he discarded.

Paul: Was it something completely new for you, to work in this high-level staff?

Schultz-Naumann: It was new for me to enter such a high-level staff. Until then I had always been at the front as a battalion adjutant, company commander or battalion commander and had served on the staff of the front headquarters. I had never served in anything higher than a division or corps, mostly divisions. Therefore, the atmosphere of a staff as high as that of the Wehrmacht Operations Staff was new to me and somewhat unreal. I received a comradely and helpful reception, particularly as I still had to use crutches to get around.

Paul: This unreality that one could experience—as I myself have experienced—if one had been a company commander in Russia and then after a couple of years at the front was posted to the staff of a division—this tense unreality contrasted with the real life that one had led until then. In my case it was not so strong, so overwhelming; but here we are talking about the

position which helped shaped the course of events in the fate
of the Reich in its last Greater German phase. Did you have
the impression that the lifestyle and comradeship in this staff
group to which you belonged resembled the image held by the
troops?

Schultz-Naumann: The lifestyle was simple. Everyone did his
duty. All of us were accommodated in simple temporary
buildings, everything was very modest. We worked in perma-
nent buildings, where two levels of cellars gave protection
against air attack. We sometimes had to use them. The comradeship which I experienced was very close. I was mostly
with officers of my age and seniority—majors and lieutenant-
colonels of the staff. It was a modest style, just as we had
known in peacetime. There were many officers there and who
had spent several years at the front. They were used to
privations and modest living.

Paul: Did you know the men you met there?

Schultz-Naumann: Yes, some I knew from the fighting in
Russia and on the front in France. I had been friends with
Major Friedel since before the war. As comrades we had been
together in 96th Infantry Regiment in Deutsch-Krone, Grenz-
mark Posen and West Prussia. Unfortunately, he was killed in
a car accident at the end of the war after he had taken part in
the German delegation under Admiral von Friedeburg in the
capitulation negotiations with Field Marshal Montgomery.

Paul: I don't mean just personal acquaintances, but more
generally: did the divisions in the field know who up there was
handling specific matters?

Schultz-Naumann: Yes, indeed, I knew of course which functions Field Marshal Keitel had as Chief of the Wehrmacht High
Command and which General Jodl had as Chief of the Wehrmacht Operations Staff. The troops also knew this.

Paul: But did one, for example, know that Colonel Poleck,
who dealt with quartermaster and supply matters, was responsible for logistics, as we call it today?

Schultz-Naumann: No, those details were known only if a commander or general staff officer at the front had a personal connection at the top. I knew Colonel Poleck in his capacity as *Oberquartiermeister* of the Wehrmacht Operations Staff. In this most critical phase of the war, he had to solve the difficult supply problems.

Paul: Apart from the Wehrmacht command, there was also at that time, especially in the Berlin area, the Nazi Party (NSDAP). In Zossen did you work together with the NSDAP of any of its organizations? Did you notice if there were any contacts established, or was it strictly an army operation?

Schultz-Naumann: There was no close cooperation except later in Berlin where Goebbels, in his capacity as Reich Defense Commissar, chose to have a say. However, the top members of the Wehrmacht Operations Staff were given insight into the so-called *"Gauleiter* Letters" by *Reichsleiter* Bormann, Chief of the Reich Chancellery and one of Hitler's confidants. They contained morale-building slogans and reported on measures against "defeatism." They often contained criticism of the Wehrmacht and mutual insults of party members. They were unworthy pamphlets. Besides this, the Party was hardly mentioned, as we had so much to do with our military tasks that there was no time for politics.

Paul: Was this work a hindrance in that you had no time for reflection, or did it give you security—working with your comrades—that transcended other things and give you the conviction that you could still contribute to an acceptable final outcome?

Schultz-Naumann: No, this security was not there. Due to Hitler's passion to know as many details as possible, the work could not be concentrated on higher-level planning or decision-making. There was no time for this. We did our duty even though we knew that the outcome had to be negative for Germany. We tried to make the best of everything. I said earlier that it all seemed unreal to me; I would like to explain this. The fiction was often maintained that we would be able to snatch victories in battles or attacks on the western, eastern, and southern fronts. But this daydreaming was especially promoted by Hitler; it influenced his closest circle and was then to be superimposed on us. This did not succeed.

Paul: Was it Hitler's concept that we had to—could—hold out between the west and east, between the Oder and the Elbe rivers? That was, was it not, the basic attitude that one might still have had then?

Schultz-Naumann: This basic attitude, of holding out between the Oder and the Elbe, or perhaps the Weser, was promoted by wishful thinking after Roosevelt's death. Naturally, the concept was around before. It was considered before the Soviet's last great offensive which began on the Oder front on April 16th.

Paul: You experienced the falling back of the western front. You also experienced the great break—if indeed there was a great break—in the Army Group concerned. Do you perhaps recall anything about the time when the Ruhr Pocket capitulated under Field Marshal Model? That was surely the last sign of the imminent end in the west.

Schultz-Naumann: There were two signs: one was the advance which crossed the Rhine over the captured bridge at Remagen; the other, which came later, was the capitulation of Army Group B with 21 German divisions in the Ruhr Pocket. Here Field Marshal Model, who despite his dedication to Hitler was basically a sober man, saw that Germany had lost and took his own life.

The collapse of the western front and the fragmentation of the German formations in the south of Germany were irreversible. In the north and northwest there was the 21st British-Canadian Army Group, commanded by the Field Marshal Montgomery; in the center, the 12th U.S. Army Group commanded by General Bradley; in the south, the 6th U.S. Army group and the First French Army under General Devers which attacked over the Rhine.

Paul: Do you know about the significance of the Allied document "Operation Eclipse"?

Schultz-Naumann: Yes, we heard about a secret document with the code name "Eclipse" in March 1945 at a strategic conference. It was also called "Operation *Sonnenfinsternis*." As was later shown by the Yalta Conference, this document dealt with splitting Germany up into zones of occupation and the treatment of Germans following an unconditional surrender. Under its terms, the Soviets were to advance up to and over the Elbe and were to receive Mecklenburg, the Province of Saxony, Anhalt, Saxony and Thuringia as their occupation zone. By the way, on the day of the capitulation, British-American forces were still in western Mecklenberg, large parts of the province of Saxony, Anhalt and western Saxony; all of Thuringia was also in their hands.

By means of a politically anticipated expansion, Stalin extended Soviet Russian power into the green heart of Germany, i.e. Thuringia, an extremely favorable strategic springboard given to him by the Western Allies in "Eclipse."

Paul: I think you mean the capture of the "Eclipse" document on April 11–12 in the Emden area which made the OKW aware of the plan.

Schultz-Naumann: No, we knew about the "Eclipse" document before March 18, 1945.

Paul: In current historical writings, April 12, 1945 is generally quoted.

Schultz-Naumann: Perhaps a second document was found then. The document I am referring to was made known to us by General Jodl in mid-March in the morning situation conference which always served to prepare the situation briefing for Hitler. The next day, however, he ordered us not to speak of it as Hitler had forbidden it.

As far as I recall, the point which led to the mentioning of the "Eclipse" theme was the fact that in mid-March the U.S. forces were pushing over the Rhine and to the east, and the target of their advance was known to be identical to a line defined in "Eclipse" as the demarcation line between the Americans and the Russians. So there was no longer any doubt as to the authenticity of this document.

Paul: Did that seem credible or were there doubts as to the authenticity of "Eclipse"?

Schultz-Naumann: Personally, I had no doubts whatsoever. I had fought against the Soviets long enough. I was the officer who most recently left the eastern front to join the staff. Yet I felt capable of analyzing this situation and its worst possible effects.

The matter is still very real for me because on Sunday, March 18, 1945, I was in Varchentin in eastern Mecklenburg to tell my wife that within eight days she would have to set off toward Hannover with the other refugees. The trigger for this was my knowledge of "Eclipse."

Paul: So you considered "Eclipse" to be a very important document?

Schultz-Naumann: Yes, the fact of its existence moved me greatly even later. It was the key to the behavior of the western and eastern armies, and especially the conduct of Hitler and the top leadership in the last weeks of the war because military events confirmed its correctness.

Although the "Eclipse" plan had originated with the British—the document was captured in a British headquarters in March—the Americans and later also the British had a bad feeling about Berlin, the capital of the Reich. Roosevelt did not originate "Eclipse." Cornelius Ryan proved this in his book *The Last Battle,* quoting documentary sources. Both the British and the Americans wanted to be the first in Berlin before the Soviet troops so that they could pull back later if needed. Montgomery had drawn up plans for a land attack and the Americans for an airborne operation to capture Berlin.

These did not come about since General Eisenhower shifted the focus of his operations to central Germany to join up with the Soviet forces on the Erfurt-Leipzig-Dresden line. He informed Stalin directly of this in his capacity as Supreme Allied Commander, a post which gave him extensive authority. He did not involve other political channels. Stalin readily agreed to this since it gave him the opportunity to capture Berlin, as subsequently in fact happened.

perhaps have construed this as wishful thinking committed to paper. It is a historical fact that very soon after the capitulation, the tension between East and West increased and the Cold War was born. But at this point, when we thought about these things and when Jodl spoke about them, one had to consider which side to back, whether West or East, because it was too early to back the West. One merely has to think about how "loyal" the West still was to its political agreements (e.g. the evacuation of the Anglo-Saxon positions in northern and central Germany in favor of the Soviets). The West was just not capable of reversing gears so quickly.

Paul: You also had foreign reports in the appendices of the War Diary. Did these numerous reports—there must even have been opinion polls in Schleswig-Holstein after the capitulation—have any influence over the course of events? In conversations between soldiers and officers, did one have the impression that one could make plans for the future or was the future a black hole for a career soldier?

Schultz-Naumann: No, it was not such a black hole because we still hoped that the Western Allies would call on us. But that was too optimistic. As more time passed and nothing of the sort happened, when the Allies were instead continually tightening the reins on the Germans—e.g. the arrest of Field Marshal Keitel and other measures—one recognized that the victors' first priority was to establish control over the vanquished.

Paul: Was there any particular tension between the OKW and the Wehrmacht Operations Staff?

Schultz-Naumann: No, after the merger of these two highest organs of command, I sensed no further tension. And the tension in the period prior to the merger has been exaggerated.

Paul: Medals were also awarded after the capitulation. I'm thinking of the oak leaf cluster to the Knight's Cross that Dönitz awarded to Jodl on May 12th. Was there a special reason for this?

Schultz-Naumann: I think that at that point Grand Admiral Dönitz wanted to honor the services which Jodl had rendered, without any public recognition, over the many years of intensive work in the High Command. And he also probably wished to reward the upright soldier that Jodl really was. I can confirm this from my own observation.

Paul: When did you last see Jodl?

Schultz-Naumann: I saw General Jodl for the last time on May 21 or 22, 1945.

Paul: What was your impression of him?

Schultz-Naumann: Jodl was a loyal soldier, whose attitude could be summed up in the phrase, "I swore my oath to Führer Adolf Hitler and I could not break it."

Paul: Were there reactions by the populace of Flensburg to the Mürwik enclave?

Schultz-Naumann: I noted no reactions by the populace. But I must say that we were so taken up with our work that we scarcely saw the inhabitants.

Paul: How many hours a day did you work?

Schultz-Naumann: It was certainly 12–16 hours a day, often more, because it was the vital task of this staff to assist the Allies and thereby help our own troops who were in captivity or rather who were being taken prisoner. There were, for example, no radio communications between the Allies and the German troops who were taken prisoner, be it in Holland or in the American sector. Units still on islands in the Aegean Sea had to be ordered back. The fortresses still being defended on the Atlantic had to receive instructions. Millions of captured German soldiers had to be moved into camps or reservations as in Schleswig-Holstein. This was only possible using the German radio and telephone communications network.

Paul: These radio communications were certainly still very useful at this time.

Schultz-Naumann: They were useful right up to the end. Not only the radio, but also the telephone. For example, when Hitler was trapped in Berlin we had telephone communications with him almost up to the moment of Berlin's collapse.

Paul: There were also numerous flights which were undertaken during and after the capitulation. Did these all take place without friction? Did they occur with the agreement of the victors? Or did everything have to be arranged under great difficulties?

Schultz-Naumann: As far as I am aware, the Allies made aircraft available for official trips they had approved.

Paul: Have you spoken with any of those gentlemen who were in Karlshorst for the second capitulation, and did they tell you anything about what happened to the German gentlemen after the ceremony?

Schultz-Naumann: I think I remember being told by Lieutenant Colonel de Maizière, who had been sent as liaison officer to Marshal Zhukov in Berlin-Karlshorst, that the Soviets were very well informed about everything that happened at the top echelon of our command. I have no information about what happened to the German officers after the capitulation ceremony.

Paul: The last days before May 23 were characterized by a Soviet political initiative which was aimed against the continued existence of Mürwik after a certain date. It is an historically proven fact that the Western Allies were very quick to fall into line with this proposal. Who do you think was responsible for this? Was it Eisenhower?

Schultz-Naumann: I have no knowledge about this.

Paul: As we now approach the conclusion of this interview, among the open questions is one concerning your role as a career officer and a member of the German general staff. Did anyone in the Wehrmacht Operations Staff have any idea that the general staff would be put on trial in Nuremberg? Was the list of war criminals, known to some in the Wehrmacht, general knowledge? Jodl and others, including Field Marshal Kluge, mentioned it. Did you know or suspect that there would be punishment, that is, not a personal punishment but punishment of the general staff as a whole? Or did you believe that those who were particularly vulnerable in this respect would have to reckon with something like this?

Schultz-Naumann: We believed the latter. I did not see these things in this way, nor did I believe that they would indict us collectively. Moreover, I was of the opinion, as were most of my comrades, that some members of the top leadership would be called to account.

Paul: You learned firsthand how history is made. Looking back after 35 years, how do you assess your activity then?

Schultz-Naumann: That question is rather difficult to answer. But when I look back at the work I did then, I must say that I would not carry out my activities any differently.

Everything I was supposed to evaluate, I did in as objective and clear a manner as possible according to the principles of the general staff, without passing judgement. I presented the facts pragmatically and endeavored to record the diary as honestly and honorably as one could expect from a German officer.

Paul: Could Percy Schramm, who kept the War Diary until April 19, 1945, have been envious when he was required to go south and had to pass on to you, a division operations officer, the materials he had accumulated? On the basis of these materials, you would now complete what Schramm could justifiably consider the crowning achievement of his career, namely to describe and record the end of the war. Did you have any contact with Percy Schramm after the war?

Schultz-Naumann: I don't think he was at all envious of me. In fact, he was very pleased that I completed the War Diary. Prior to the publication of the German edition of *The Last Thirty Days* I wrote to him asking for his approval. He agreed and said he was very pleased that somebody was going to write about the end of the war in the unprejudiced style of an unbiased military observer.

I also had contact with him later, before his history of the war *(Kriegstagebuch des Oberkommandos der Wehrmacht)* was published in four double volumes. I gave him a copy of my original documents; the originals I gave to the German Federal Archives. My copy of the War Diary is the virtual original, even though it is only a copy, since the real original was probably burned by British soldiers in the confusion during the capture of Flensburg-Müwik.

Paul: The volumes of appendices exist in the military archives of the German Federal Archives, and this could be regarded as a stroke of luck for your work. There was a War Diary of the Army High Command, which is also contained in the military archives. However, as the Army High Command was merged with the Armed Forces High Command on April 24, 1945, the question arises as to who kept the Army High Command War Diary. Did you ever meet this person?

Schultz-Naumann: There certainly must have been a recorder of the Army High Command War Diary, but I never met him because the Army High Command was independent. When we were combined on April 24 during the evacuation to Flensburg, the issue was never mentioned.

Paul: You left the Mürwik enclave on May 23, 1945 and you must have taken this copy with you. Presumably it was a carbon copy which your secretary had typed, since you yourself did not type.

Schultz-Naumann: It was my secretary, Miss Jaehnke. Both she and I made a legal declaration before the first publication of the book that I compiled the War Diary and she typed it.

Paul: Would you tell us how you came to leave your duty station in the Mürwik enclave on Monday, May 23 just before its dissolution?

Schultz-Naumann: That is very simple. In the days prior to May 23, 1945, I was in a poor state of health since the stump of my amputated leg had become inflamed and I had to be hospitalized. (I had lost my leg in the battles during the invasion of France.) As the hospitals in Flensburg were overcrowded, I received a pass signed by the commander in Flensburg, Brigadier (Brigadier General) Churcher, which authorized me to cross the Kaiser Wilhelm Canal and go to Hamburg.

I did this as early as possible on May 23, to start hospital treatment as soon as possible.

Looking back on it now, a sixth sense told me to take a copy of the War Diary with me, naturally without the appendices. To come back to your earlier question as to whether I was aware of the historic significance of my work, I suppose the answer is yes; otherwise, I would not have taken it with me. And that is how the War Diary was saved. I actually left it with an acquaintance who had a farm near Kiel; I stopped by briefly on my drive and told him that I would pick it up later. And that is how the War Diary was saved.

Paul: You recovered it some months or years later?

Schultz-Naumann: I picked it up a year or two later, I can't remember exactly, when I was working as a taxi driver and made several runs from Niedersachsen to Schleswig-Holstein.

Index

All geographic locations and all armed service corps, divisions, groups, etc., are presumed to be German unless otherwise indicated.

About the Author

Joachim Schultz-Naumann, born in Malchin (Mecklenburg-Schwerin), studied economics and history. In 1934 he became a professional soldier. He fought in Poland, France, Russia and Italy. He was a senior staff officer (G3) in various infantry combat divisions and was gravely wounded several times. Having lost a leg towards the end of the war, Major Schultz-Naumann, a trained military historian, was assigned to keep the official War Diary of the German High Command. After the War, he was among the first officers attached to NATO. He gave up his military career to become a business executive. He maintains a professional interest in writing military history.

Eisenhower tried to avoid heavy losses of his own forces by avoiding the conquest of Berlin which he—as a soldier's general and not as a political general—preferred to leave to his Soviet allies. From his viewpoint, therefore, Berlin was not decisive. There was no Allied political directive to take Berlin, even though Churchill and Montgomery were both pushing for it once they learned Eisenhower had relinquished Berlin to Stalin.

Paul: We come now to the division of the command staff into North and South; they were split on April 20th.

Schultz-Naumann: Yes, the command staff was divided that day. Those parts of the Wehrmacht Operations Staff that were not absolutely essential to conduct the battle for Berlin were sent to southern Germany. Among them was also the recorder of the War Diary of the OKW, Major Percy Schramm. They were also looking for a liaison officer for Grand Admiral Dönitz from the Wehrmacht Operations Staff, and I volunteered.

Paul: You went straight to Plön?

Schultz-Naumann: No, we had to leave Zossen on April 20 because Marshal Konev was moving in. The staff then moved into the Reich Air Defense School in Wannsee. I managed to leave Berlin on April 22, because Berlin was encircled on April 24, 1945.

Some days later after I reported to Plön, it was realized that the War Diary had not been kept at the OKW since April 20, 1945, since Major Schramm had been sent to southern Germany. The decisive events, however, took place in northern Germany and especially in Berlin.

Paul: At this point, the command group with Keitel and Jodl had already arrived in Flensburg-Mürwik?

Schultz-Naumann: Yes, the Wehrmacht Operations Staff was located in Mürwik, as well as my chief in the Operations Section Army West, Colonel Meyer-Detring. He gave me the task of writing the War Diary retroactively, starting April 20, 1945.

Paul: For a war diary one needs documents; they are the raw material. General Jodl, when the OKW moved out of Berlin, was very keen that even the smallest note, the most insignificant order should be taken along in order to have them available to record history. Thus, we can crudely say that the last "red tape" of the Wehrmacht Operations Staff arrived completely intact in Mürwik and was later surrendered to the British. You now had to sift all these documents concerning events since April 20th. How did you do this?

Schultz-Naumann: I received permission to do this by visiting the various departments and collecting the documents, i.e. the originals of directives, orders, and reports. I collected them all, evaluated them, and from them constructed the War Diary starting April 20, 1945. I worked undisturbed in a temporary building. I was given a secretary for the actual writing. The "safe" for the War Diary and its supporting appendices was my officer's war chest, which also contained my luggage and other things.

Paul: Did you realize what you were doing? That you were the first contemporary historian in the writing of this history, a historian as Major Percy Schramm understood it, or was it for you just an interesting and important task, part of your duty?

Schultz-Naumann: For me, it was initially simply an interesting, important task and part of my duty. However, as I was interested in history, it was also enjoyable, insofar as one could talk of joy under the prevailing circumstances. At the beginning, I was not as aware of the actual historic significance of this documentation as I was at the end, after the capitulation. The things which I heard at the situation conferences—which continued to be held in the old style after May 8th—the events which occurred and the problems which appeared gave me some indication of the historic significance of my writing.

Paul: Who was there? For Percy Schramm it was General Warlimont and then General Winter, both successive chiefs of the Wehrmacht Operations Staff, who told him what had happened at the situation conferences. Who was your informant?

Schultz-Naumann: I had been involved in all the events since the beginning of May, so I was up to date. From then on, I kept the War Diary daily as I was always present at the situation conferences.

Paul: And after the capitulation? Did you take shorthand?

Schultz-Naumann: I was present at the situation conferences as soon as Keitel and Jodl arrived in Mürwik. That was May 3, 1945. Situation conferences were also held in the first days of May. I was called to attend them; I did not take shorthand, I could not, but I could jot things down very quickly and I always reviewed my notes immediately after the situation conference.

Paul: You also experienced the Baltic rescue operations from your position in Mürwik. Have you any specific memories?

Schultz-Naumann: Certainly. The sea evacuation filled us all—and especially me as recorder of the War Diary since I wrote about it—with satisfaction and pride due to the fact that our navy had managed to save so many Germans, both soldiers and civilians.

Paul: Did you speak with Colonel Meyer-Detring after he returned from his flight to Army Group Schörner in Bohemia?

Schultz-Naumann: I remember that the Colonel gave us details after his return. It was his task to deliver the terms of the capitulation. Thus, protected by an American escort, he passed through the areas controlled by Czech insurgents and reached Prague. He was treated correctly by the Americans. He was impressed by the will to resist shown by the troops there. In Prague they wanted to launch a counterattack. Due to the conclusion of the capitulation, this did not happen. Incidentally, some units which wanted to break out to the west carried on fighting in Czechoslovakia even after the capitulation.

Paul: In the situation in which you found yourself on May 9— you knew what had happened, what had been ordered from Flensburg-Mürwik, and that the capitulation was in effect—

did you have the impression that Mürwik was still somewhat effective? Or was there the feeling that after the arrival of the British it was all over?

Schultz-Naumann: No, not at all. I had the impression that one tried to remain operational. That could also be seen in that the British and the Americans—the commander of the Allied Commission was U.S. General Rooks—wanted to use the German High Command to achieve an orderly implementation of the capitulation.

Paul: This certainly complied with an aim that was also held by the German headquarters. A book by an American historian maintains that Churchill saw a possibility in using the German units—which stayed together for a certain period in captivity— for future operations, perhaps against the East. In the period up to May 23, 1945, did you witness anything which may have supported this view?

Schultz-Naumann: I would not like to put it in the same way as that Anglo-Saxon writer did. That is too speculative for me. The German side, as was known, wanted the Western Allies to turn against the Soviets. Beyond that, there was the German desire that the Western Allies would use German troops for this purpose, even if they had been disarmed and held in captivity. But in purely private conversations with Allied officers up to the rank of commanding general, especially on the British side, these matters were not mentioned.

Paul: There is one remarkable thing which may have been used as an indicator by an historian born after the event: the OKW operations maps. In the latter phase, in the second and third weeks of May, these large maps, which were redrawn twice a day, carried the German, British, and American units shown together so that one could sense at a glance what German military potential the Western Allies might call on. Do you know about these maps?

Schultz-Naumann: Probably so. If they were drawn to show the German potential—the potential of captured German soldiers—together with the Anglo-Saxon units, then one could